YOGHURT

Edible

Series Editor: Andrew F. Smith

EDIBLE is a revolutionary series of books dedicated to food and drink that explores the rich history of cuisine. Each book reveals the global history and culture of one type of food or beverage.

Already published

Apple Erika Janik, *Avocado* Jeff Miller, *Banana* Lorna Piatti-Farnell, *Barbecue* Jonathan Deutsch and Megan J. Elias, *Beans* Nathalie Rachel Morris, *Beef* Lorna Piatti-Farnell, *Beer* Gavin D. Smith, *Berries* Heather Arndt Anderson, *Biscuits and Cookies* Anastasia Edwards, *Brandy* Becky Sue Epstein, *Bread* William Rubel, *Cabbage* Meg Muckenhoupt, *Cake* Nicola Humble, *Caviar* Nichola Fletcher, *Champagne* Becky Sue Epstein, *Cheese* Andrew Dalby, *Chillies* Heather Arndt Anderson, *Chocolate* Sarah Moss and Alexander Badenoch, *Cocktails* Joseph M. Carlin, *Coffee* Jonathan Morris, *Corn* Michael Owen Jones, *Curry* Colleen Taylor Sen, *Dates* Nawal Nasrallah, *Doughnut* Heather Delancey Hunwick, *Dumplings* Barbara Gallani, *Edible Flowers* Constance L. Kirker and Mary Newman, *Eggs* Diane Toops, *Fats* Michelle Phillipov, *Figs* David C. Sutton, *Foie Gras* Norman Kolpas, *Game* Paula Young Lee, *Gin* Lesley Jacobs Solmonson, *Hamburger* Andrew F. Smith, *Herbs* Gary Allen, *Herring* Kathy Hunt, *Honey* Lucy M. Long, *Hot Dog* Bruce Kraig, *Ice Cream* Laura B. Weiss, *Jam, Jelly and Marmalade* Sarah B. Hood, *Lamb* Brian Yarvin, *Lemon* Toby Sonneman, *Lobster* Elisabeth Townsend, *Melon* Sylvia Lovegren, *Milk* Hannah Velten, *Moonshine* Kevin R. Kosar, *Mushroom* Cynthia D. Bertelsen, *Mustard* Demet Güzey, *Nuts* Ken Albala, *Offal* Nina Edwards, *Olive* Fabrizia Lanza, *Onions and Garlic* Martha Jay, *Oranges* Clarissa Hyman, *Oyster* Carolyn Tillie, *Pancake* Ken Albala, *Pasta and Noodles* Kantha Shelke, *Pickles* Jan Davison, *Pie* Janet Clarkson, *Pineapple* Kaori O'Connor, *Pizza* Carol Helstosky, *Pomegranate* Damien Stone, *Pork* Katharine M. Rogers, *Potato* Andrew F. Smith, *Pudding* Jeri Quinzio, *Rice* Renee Marton, *Rum* Richard Foss, *Saffron* Ramin Ganeshram, *Salad* Judith Weinraub, *Salmon* Nicolaas Mink, *Sandwich* Bee Wilson, *Sauces* Maryann Tebben, *Sausage* Gary Allen, *Seaweed* Kaori O'Connor, *Shrimp* Yvette Florio Lane, *Soup* Janet Clarkson, *Spices* Fred Czarra, *Sugar* Andrew F. Smith, *Sweets and Candy* Laura Mason, *Tea* Helen Saberi, *Tequila* Ian Williams, *Tomato* Clarissa Hyman, *Truffle* Zachary Nowak, *Vanilla* Rosa Abreu-Runkel, *Vodka* Patricia Herlihy, *Water* Ian Miller, *Whiskey* Kevin R. Kosar, *Wine* Marc Millon, *Yoghurt* June Hersh

Yoghurt

A Global History

June Hersh

REAKTION BOOKS

Published by Reaktion Books Ltd
Unit 32, Waterside
44–48 Wharf Road
London N1 7UX, UK
www.reaktionbooks.co.uk

First published 2021
Copyright © June Hersh 2021

Printed and bound in India by Replika Press Pvt. Ltd

A catalogue record for this book is available from the British Library

ISBN 978 1 78914 412 3

Contents

Introduction
Yoghurt: A Food Fad Trending for Millennia

Few foods can claim to have been consumed as early as 10,000 BCE and to have sustained enough popularity in the thousands of years since to remain a kitchen staple today. Even fewer could be called plain, tart or sour and have those pejorative terms considered to be compliments. However, those statements hold true for one of the world's oldest fermented foods: yoghurt.

Yoghurt is one of the most pliable and versatile foods, serving not only as an ingredient or condiment, but as a stand-alone meal. It can be eaten at breakfast, lunch or dinner and makes for a healthy snack and delectable dessert. It pairs well with both savoury and sweet add-ins and is enjoyed across the globe with a spoon, a straw or as a frozen confection. It is simple to prepare at home and, for some, making it is a ritual of weekly practice. It has proven health claims that take it from being a super food, which has nutritional benefits, to a functional food with a bonanza of value-added characteristics. Yoghurt is feeding and fuelling populations in every corner of the world with the nutrient-dense benefits of milk, without the side effects suffered by those who are lactose-intolerant.

To better understand the impact of yoghurt, you need to understand its healthy characteristics. As Robert Hutkins explains in his book *Microbiology and Technology of Fermented Foods* (2006), when a food is fermented, as yoghurt is, its raw materials are converted through the action of microbes. Microbes are what transform grapes into wine or soybeans into tempeh and miso. What makes these fermented foods so valuable are the billions of live microbes, good bacteria that you are ingesting and introducing to your gut. Because these microbes confer a benefit to the host, they are considered 'probiotic' (from the Greek word for 'life'). And while, Hutkins admits, they are often merely visitors, when consumed regularly, they can compete with bad bacteria, produce vitamins and help modulate your immune system.

Yoghurt was a transformative food for Neolithic people and became the foundation of many of the world's first collective communities. While Neolithic people undoubtedly didn't have the level of sophistication needed to understand the complex process of fermentation, they found that when they ate foods such as yoghurt, they felt better and stronger. It is no surprise, therefore, that yoghurt is mentioned and revered in the ancient religious scripts of almost every world

Curds in a traditional Indian Manipuri pot.

religion, is the subject of exhaustive archaeological findings and can be found in the theoretical writings of classical Greek and Roman scholars.

As it proliferated in the diet of many residing in Central Asia, yoghurt became an important ingredient during the Golden Age of Islam, and recipes featuring it were integral to the world's oldest cookbooks. In the late 1800s and early 1900s, yoghurt became the focus of many scientific studies, and the prescient writings from ancient scientists were being tested and proven in labs throughout the world. When yoghurt's health halo was firmly affixed, it was the topic of news stories across the globe, and yoghurt for medicinal purposes was all the rage. The twentieth century saw yoghurt move from a pharmaceutical product to an indispensable member of the supermarket dairy aisle as manufacturers seized on its momentum and ushered in the age of yoghurt's commercialization.

Yoghurt wars between major producers in the late twentieth and early twenty-first centuries were hard-fought, and consumers then had a plethora of choices and varieties to choose from. In 2016 yoghurt sales worldwide reached U.S.$77 billion, and are forecast to top $100 billion by 2023. Major yoghurt producers recognize that consumers today are looking for the most probiotic bang for their buck, with new and interesting flavours, plant-based alternatives and varieties designed for fast-paced lifestyles. These factors appeal especially to a burgeoning Chinese and Southeast Asian market. Numerous studies point to yoghurt's health benefits and consider it a signature foodstuff for a healthy diet and lifestyle. Compared with those who do not eat yoghurt, yoghurt eaters are 'generally healthier, leaner, more highly educated and of a higher socio-economic status'.[1] Studies go on to show that yoghurt eaters are more likely to be women, to read labels, to be more physically active and more aware of the links between food and health, while less likely to smoke or drink or go to fast food restaurants. If that isn't enough, they tend to have an overall better health-related quality of life and mental-health outlook. Scientific studies into the health benefits of yoghurt additionally find a positive correlation between yoghurt consumers and a lower risk for cardiovascular disease, type 2 diabetes and obesity. Today's yoghurt eaters want indulgence without guilt, the choice of their daily fix of dairy or wholesome nutrition without animal products and, of course, sweetness without sugar. As a BBC news report observed, 'In half a century, the humble yoghurt has gone from hippy health food to mass market phenomenon, triggered a functional food revolution and became a multi-billion-pound industry.'[2] How amazing to think that an ancient global food phenomenon is still thriving and expanding to satisfy such a growing market demand across the world.

I

Back to the Future

We only have to go back to the Neolithic period, or New Stone Age, the final stage of cultural evolution and technological development among prehistoric humans, to trace the roots of the functional food that is yoghurt. It is believed that Neolithic people between 10,000 and 6500 BCE in Anatolia (modern-day Turkey) were moving from a hunter-gatherer society towards dairy farming and domesticating animals.

Camels, yaks, cows, horses, llamas, sheep and goats once valued for their meat were now being utilized to provide sustenance through milking. Early people found themselves with an abundance of fresh milk, but there was just one problem – they were lactose-intolerant. Luckily for them, Mother Nature donned her white lab coat and created protocooperation, an organic synergy between the forces of heat and bacteria, working together to convert milk into an easily digestible source of nourishment. She took fresh milk – chock-full of protein and calcium as well as phosphorous; riboflavin; vitamins B6, B12 and D; potassium and magnesium – and inoculated it with the bacteria that were ever-present in the environment. She then brought the sunshine, which created enough heat to activate the good bacteria and, like Pac-Man, they consumed the lactose (natural milk

Nicolaes Pieterszoon Berchem, *Woman Milking a Ewe*, 19th century, oil on canvas. Moving from a hunter-gatherer society to one where animals were domesticated and used for their dairy products helped lead to the discovery of yoghurt.

sugar), created lactic acid and fermented the milk. The milk proteins broke down (denatured) and then over time came back together and coagulated. Her chemistry experiment created an entirely new food packed with live and active healthy microorganisms, with a tart and tangy flavour and a thick and curdled texture. That is why most consider the word 'yoghurt' to be derived from the Turkish word *yoğurmak*, which translates as 'thickened, curdled or coagulated'.

So how did Neolithic man learn to harness the power of Mother Nature to create yoghurt? It was more a serendipitous effort than a learnt one, with two viable theories. The first suggests that herdsmen stored milk from their freshly milked animals in bags fashioned from intestinal gut. Over time, the natural bacterial enzymes in these bags fermented the milk and created yoghurt. A second theory posits that the earliest dairy farmers would store their fresh milk in containers that sat in the hot sun. Bacteria from nearby trees and plants infiltrated the milk and, as evolutionary geneticist Mark Thomas noted, 'if you milked a cow in the morning . . . in the Near East by lunchtime [the milk] would have started to ferment into yogurt.'[1]

This remarkable discovery of how to convert milk into a near-lactose-free, long-lasting and nutrient-dense food source was considered by scholars such as Joachim Burger, an evolutionary anthropologist at the University of Mainz in Germany, to be 'a transformative development in human history'. Burger initiated the EU project BEAN (bridging the European and Anatolian Neolithic) and in that context stated, 'The processing of milk to make cheese and yogurt contributed significantly to the development of dairy farming . . . making a valuable foodstuff available to the human population.'[2]

There is concrete, or should we say, 'clay' evidence showing that the Neoliths were fermenting their milk and achieving a high level of sophistication with their overall culinary skills. Julie Dunne, an archaeological scientist at the University of

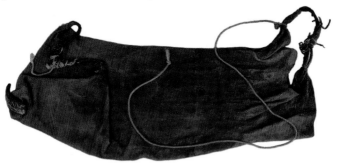

Goat-skin bag (qirbah or sqa) used to carry and churn milk products, Bedouin culture, Oman, 1970s, suggestive of what Neolithic herdsmen might have fashioned.

Bristol, studied residue on 81 ancient pottery remnants from the Libyan Sahara and found 'the chemical signatures were unambiguously from animal fats'.[3] They were able to identify the remains of dairy products made from the milks of cows, goats and sheep dating as far back as 5000 BCE. This finding confirms the theory that vessels were certainly being used to hold milk and that as far back as Neolithic times, those not possessing the genetic mutation to digest milk were likely making cheese and yoghurt rather than drinking milk directly from their animals. Andrew Curry takes this one step further, in his article entitled 'Archaeology: The Milk Revolution', citing another find near central Poland on which archaeologists came across fragments suspected to have been left behind by some of Europe's oldest farmers.[4] The pottery was dotted with tiny holes as if the clay had been deliberately perforated. Geochemists from the UK examined the pieces and found signatures of milk fat, which they extrapolated to

Terracotta hemispherical strainer, Lydian culture, 6th century BCE, which may have been used to prepare a cheese- or yoghurt-like food.

mean that these ancient dairy farmers were not only storing milk to ferment but had developed a method of separating curd from whey (the yellowish liquid that remains after the formation of curds), thereby turning their milk into yoghurt or cheese.

A confirmation of this was discovered at Durrington Walls, a major Neolithic settlement dating to around 2500 BCE and located just 3 kilometres (2 mi.) northeast of Stonehenge. Examination by a collaborative team of archaeologists from various UK universities in 2015 revealed that dairy product residue from cottage cheese, yoghurt and curds and whey was found in pots at the site. Additionally, many of those found to have dairy residue were located near the ceremonial monuments, which indicated that dairy products such as milk and yoghurt had a religious significance to these burgeoning societies. The authors of the study were impressed at the sophistication in these communities and the high level of what they termed 'culinary organization'.[5]

A transformative use of yoghurt showing innovation and adaptation was when Neolithic man created what might have been one of the world's first recipes. No longer sedentary, people needed a food that had an extended shelf life and was easily portable. These early chefs prepared a product that was the perfect marriage of their two most abundant natural resources: cracked wheat or barley and yoghurt. This mixture, which was called *kashk* or *kishke*, depending on which region you resided in, had a dough-like consistency and would be salted and then placed in porous vessels to drain. After several days or up to two weeks, the mixture would thicken and then be laid out in the hot sun to remove any remaining moisture. After another week, it would be crumbled into small balls, which could be reconstituted with little more than water and fire.

Dried yoghurt balls (*kashk*) at Chorsu Bazaar, Tashkent, Uzbekistan.

These nomads made their way through Central Asia, touching the entire region from Iran to Turkey, from the Balkans to Afghanistan and south to India and Pakistan. They continued their wanderings into Europe and brought with them their new-found techniques and culinary know-how. Versions of kashk and kishke appeared in the repertoire of many inhabitants of the area: it was known as *jameed* in Jordan, *quroot* in Afghanistan or *tarhana* in Turkey. This same ancient food made its way to Eastern European Ashkenazi households and was known as *kasha*, or *kishke*, depending on its preparation. A dish called *kkishkiyya* was found in a tenth-century Baghdad cookbook and was said to be a cure for a hangover. A hearty combination of meat, chickpeas and vegetables would meld with kashk to alleviate both headache and stomach-ache. Marco Polo, in his fourteenth-century diary, which recounted his travels through Mongolia and his observations of the great army of Genghis Khan, noted that the Mongols 'have likewise their milk dried into a species of paste, which, when about to use, they stir till it becomes liquid and can be drunk.' Khan recognized the sustaining properties of yoghurt, and long before Napoleon was quoted as saying 'an army marches on its stomach', Genghis Khan was proving it to be true. Kashk is still used today, in liquid form to add a funky cheesy flavour to a dish, or ground into a very fine powder, which has an indefinite shelf life.

Ancient Wisdom

The Neolithic period was a great time of discovery and humankind continued to evolve for centuries in both thought and lifestyle, with yoghurt remaining an important food source. By the fifth and fourth centuries BCE Greek scholars were reporting on just about every discipline imaginable, from military tactics to pharmaceuticals, and their theories and observations have, in many instances, stood the test of time. Without the aid of social media, yoghurt managed to earn an important spot in the conversation of digestion and gut health among these classical thinkers. Hippocrates, the 'father of medicine', and Herodotus, the 'father of history', were two such influencers. Hippocrates' biomedical methodology still stands today, and in his treatise 'Application of Hygienic and Dietary Measures', he touted the merits of yoghurt. Herodotus spent his life travelling throughout the Persian region collecting what he termed 'personal inquiries'. He wrote about a food with the qualities and structure of yoghurt that he considered to be a gift from the Thracians.

As the first century unfolded, Roman naturalist Pliny the Elder (Gaius Plinius Secundus) penned his historic work *Natural History*. In the sections focusing on medicine and drugs, he mentions that some nomadic tribes knew how to 'thicken the milk into a substance with an agreeable acidity'.

'Physician Preparing an Elixir', folio from an Arabic translation of
Dioscorides' *Materia Medica* of 1224 CE.

Pliny noted that the yoghurt of the Assyrians was called *lebeny*
(meaning 'life'), which they regarded as a divine food as well
as an indispensable remedy for most illnesses. His contemporary, Dioscorides, a Greek pharmacist, wrote the legendary
work on medicine and pharmacology entitled *De materia*

medica. In it, he too discussed yoghurt as a way to cleanse the body of impurities and treat tuberculosis.

The investigations into yoghurt's health benefits continued into the second century, when Galen of Pergamon, a Greek physician and philosopher, expanded on some of Hippocrates' theories. He noted a drink that could purify bilious and burning stomachs. This drink was most likely *pyriate* or *oxygala* (*oxi* meant 'sour', *gala* 'milk'), a drink that Susanna Hoffman notes in her book *The Olive and the Caper*, 'was known to Greeks since classical times' and continued to influence medical practices through the seventeenth century.[6]

Not Lost in Translation

Yoghurt's popularity did not wane as the world moved from ancient thought to medieval practice in the fifth to fifteenth centuries. While much of the world was experiencing tumult, in what some would call the Dark Ages, the Arab world was experiencing an awakening. As the caliphs were building more advanced cities and moving the heart of the Arab world to Baghdad, the Abbasid Empire was placing a premium on the words of ancient thinkers.

During this Islamic Golden Age, translating the works of Greek and Roman scholars was all the rage. One of the most prominent translators was Hunayn ibn Ishaq, a ninth-century physician and scientist called the 'father of Islamic medicine'. In addition to translating, he wrote a number of his own treatises, wherein he wrote of *laban* (yoghurt or sour milk). He theorized that laban can strengthen the stomach, cure diarrhoea, produce appetite, regulate the heat of the blood, purify the humours, and make blood more fluid, while giving a fresh and healthy colour to the skin, lips and mucous membranes.

Another voice was that of Rhazes, a Persian who served as the chief physician of Baghdad. While an admirer of Galen, he disagreed with him on many of his more speculative theories. However, one topic they did agree on was yoghurt. Rhazes saw yoghurt as a refreshing source of nourishment and suggested that it should be consumed for persons in whom ordinary milk curdles in the stomach and produces anxiety or feelings of heaviness in the stomach, or causes unconsciousness. Might Rhazes have been the first to make the mind–gut connection, which posits a direct communication link between the microbes in your gut and your brain?

Not to be bested by Arab translators, two Turks active in the eleventh century, Mahmud Kashgari and Yusuf Has Hajib, are credited with the first unequivocal definitions of yoghurt in the world's oldest dictionaries. In *Diwan Lughat al-Turk* (Compendium of Turkic Dialects) and *Kutadgu Bilig* (roughly translated to mean 'Wisdom of Royal Glory'), both men referenced yoghurt specifically and its importance to nomadic Turks. These scholarly works helped to spread the health benefits of yoghurt throughout the Levant, a geographic area that encompassed the westernmost tip of Asia and Turkey.

Baghdad Cookery

Unfortunately, only a couple of treasured cookbooks focusing on Baghdad cookery survived the ravages of time, among them *Kitāb al-ṭabīkh* (Book of Cookery) penned by Ibn Sayyar al-Warraq and a later compendium known as the *Book of Dishes* by Muhammad ibn al-Hasan ibn al-Karim. These pre-eminent cookbooks were written between the tenth and twelfth centuries and included recipes that graced the banquet tables of the great caliphs. The recipes have been lovingly translated

Middle Eastern aubergine and meat stew on a bed of yoghurt.

and shared by several authors, including Lilia Zaouali in her book *Medieval Cuisine of the Islamic World* (2007). One dish, *labaniyya rūmiyya*, is a Greek or Byzantine stew in which meat is parboiled with chopped chard leaves, and a pound of yoghurt and a half *ūqiya* (an ancient measurement) of rice are added to the pot to create a silky sauce and foundation for the stew.

In Maxime Rodinson, A. J. Arberry and Charles Perry's *Medieval Arab Cookery* (2001), a variety of yoghurt recipes from the earliest Arabic cookbooks are cited, including a yoghurt relish and a recipe for *qar'bi-laban* (gourds with yoghurt). The process includes peeling, removing the seeds and cutting up aubergines (eggplant) prior to boiling them in salted water. Once they are fully cooked and then air dried, they are mixed with Persian yoghurt, garlic and nigella (a tiny black seed with a pungent onion taste). As the author of the original recipe states, 'It comes out excellently.'

The best representations of Baghdad cookery often paired yoghurt with aubergine and meat, such as *Burani-ye bademjun*, connected to Būrān, the wife of the Caliph al Ma'mūn, purportedly prepared for her wedding feast. In *Medieval Arab Cookery*, a recipe for *Burani-ye bademjun* features the balance of hot and cold, with the spices of harissa, coriander and cassia (Chinese) cinnamon being tamed by the cooling yoghurt. Aubergine fried in sesame-flavoured oil benefits from the acidity and sour notes from yoghurt, which also serves to cut the fat from the meatballs which are fried in tail fat. The yoghurt makes the dish more easily digestible.

> Fry eggplants [aubergines] in sesame oil or fresh tail fat and peel them and put them in a capacious vessel. Then pound them with the ladle until they become like pounded harissa. Then you throw on Persian yoghurt in which you have put garlic pounded with a little salt and mixed it well with it. Then take pounded lean meat and make meatballs from it and throw them in the tail fat, and put them on the surface of the eggplants and yoghurt (sc. after frying). You sprinkle dry coriander and Chinese cinnamon on it, both pounded fine, and it comes out well.

From earliest times, when humanity realized the benefits of utilizing natural resources for sustained nourishment, through the days of Baghdad's glorious cooking, yoghurt put down its cultural, nutritional and medicinal roots, which germinated in the centuries to come.

2
'Yoghurtism':
A Religious Experience

Many of the world's most prominent religions, including Judaism, Christianity, Sikhism, Jainism, Buddhism, Hinduism and Islam, have put their faith in yoghurt. There are a host of references to yoghurt in ancient religious texts, including Indian Ayurvedic scripts, the Bible, the Talmud, the Koran and Buddhist writings. It is evident by these references that culinary influences of the day were making their way into religious writings and rituals. As yoghurt was a prevalent food in the regions where many of these texts were penned, and stories of yoghurt's benefits were topics of discussion, it is no wonder that we find many mentions of it throughout religious scripture.

You could say that yoghurt plays a role of biblical proportions in the Old Testament, with many references to curds (an interchangeable term for yoghurt and sour milk). In Genesis 18:8, it is written that when guests came to visit Abraham's tent, he 'took curds and milk and the calf that he had prepared, and set it before them'. Persian writings and legends from that time suggest Abraham owed his fecundity and longevity to these curds. In Isaiah 7:15, it says, 'He shall eat curds and honey when he knows how to refuse the evil and choose good . . . he will eat curds, for everyone that is left within the land will eat curds and honey.'

Proverbs 30:33 says, 'For pressing milk produces curds, pressing the nose produces blood, and pressing anger produces strife.' References in Judges, in which curds were served in a 'lordly bowl' and in 2 Samuel, in which David and his exhausted followers were offered honey and curds, only serve to cement the idea that curds were a staple in the diet of the Israelites. These references make you wonder if instead of being called the land of milk and honey, Israel should more aptly have been called the land of yoghurt and honey.

The Koran does not mention yoghurt or curds per se, but in discussing the blessed Sunnah (the way of the prophet Muhammed) foods, a traditional barley dish called *talbina*, a derivative of the Arabic word *laban* (referring to a thickened yoghurt), is referenced. It was so named as the finished dish resembles creamy yoghurt, and can often include yoghurt as an ingredient. The dish is said to be a cure for sadness and a mainstay offering served after a funeral: 'At-talbina gives rest to the heart of the patient and makes it active and relieves some of his sorrow and grief.' An ancient recipe reveals that it is made by mixing two spoons of barley and a cup of water and cooking for five minutes, before a cup of yoghurt and honey is added.

Yoghurt is still one of the essential foods in Islamic tradition, eaten to break the Ramadan fast, as well as a mainstay in many dishes, such as biryani, a holiday stew that takes its name from the Persian meaning 'fried before cooking', or *bolani*, an Afghan stuffed flatbread, enjoyed on the first day of Eid al-Adha, also known as the Festival of the Sacrifice.

In both the Bible and the Koran, there are strict dietary laws in place; however, the avoidance of mixing milk and meat was practised by those of the Jewish faith who interpreted the Bible in a particular way, but was not a factor in the diet of those of the Muslim faith who follow the Koran. Mark

Talbina can be served either thick as porridge or in the Aleppo style shown here: barley soup swimming with yoghurt.

Kurlansky notes in his comprehensive book *Milk! A 10,000-year Food Fracas*, that while the Jews influenced Muslim dietary habits, Muslims never adopted the Jewish custom of not mixing milk and meat. In fact, many recipes of the time used 'Persian milk', as yoghurt was often referred to, as a marinade for meat. However, that is not the only religious implication when considering yoghurt. It is certainly possible that in ancient times, yoghurt was made from the milk of a pig or camel. In the archaeological findings previously discussed, porcine fat was routinely found in milk vessels. However, if you follow the laws of kashruth (meaning kosher-fit, or proper), neither the pig nor the camel is acceptable, as neither is a ruminant, nor does either animal have cloven hooves. According to halal food practice (Islamic foods that are lawful and permissible), the pig is forbidden. Therefore, these dietary laws also governed which animals could be used for their milk and in turn for fermenting milk into yoghurt. Followers of kosher and halal customs need to be mindful of whether a yoghurt includes gelatin or rennet, as those additives can sometimes be derived from forbidden sources. Today you can look for seals of approval to help weed out the non-kosher and non-halal products.

References to yoghurt can be seen in writings as well as symbols found in Buddhist tantras dating back to medieval India. Yoghurt is regarded as a pure food, white in colour, free of negativism, the process of making yoghurt being seen as a metaphor for transforming the spirit. An annual festival held in Tibetan China celebrates yoghurt. Aptly named *Shoton* or *Sho Dun*, Tibetan for 'yoghurt banquet', this festival, which originated about five hundred years ago, was originally religious in origin, as laymen would bring yoghurt to the monks after a long period of meditation. The celebration is observed late in the sixth or early in the seventh month of the Tibetan calendar (generally August/September). It involves an interesting mix of eating yoghurt and watching opera and traditional dance performances, as well as other colourful activities and displays, including the unveiling of the thangka (a religious-inspired painting on fabric). Yoghurt is enjoyed in many forms, with one popular bar in the capital city of Lhasa serving more than 1,000 bowls of yoghurt a day.

Indian Ayurvedic scripts dating back to the Vedic period of 1500–500 BCE are filled with references to curds and honey, often termed 'the food of the Gods'. *Madhuparka*, a mixture of curds and honey, was often served to distinguished guests and visitors and reserved for special occasions. In Sanskrit writings, 'sour milk' is repeatedly mentioned, and reference is often made to *dadhi*, a fermented milk. It is considered to be a cooling food and one of the five nectars of the *panchamrita* (*panchamrit, panchamrut*) used in Hindu worship still today.

Dr Vasant Lad, who practises Ayurvedic medicine, notes that yoghurt is the only fermented food considered *sattvic*

Unveiling of the thangka is a significant part of the yoghurt festival (Shoton) in Tibet. Photograph taken at Drepung Monastery, Lhasa, August 2010.

(nourishing and providing balance). Based on the ancient texts, he suggests you do not eat yoghurt in excess in the spring or winter or consume it at night, as these are *kapha* times, when adverse effects are increased. He continues to suggest you should be mindful of incompatible food combinations with yoghurt such as lemons, nightshades or hot drinks and consume it in moderation, as too much could block your *srotas* (circulatory channels).

Yoghurt holds a unique position for Sikhs, as a sacred component of their burial ritual. Sikhism originated in the fifteenth century in the Punjab region of India. Today it is practised by more than 20 million people worldwide. Although Sikhs are cremated, prior to that final act the body is purified with a mixture of water and yoghurt. The yoghurt is allowed to dry before the dead are wrapped in burial clothing. Some feel the white colour and the natural properties provide cleansing and imbue holiness.

Breaking from religions in which yoghurt is revered and embraced, in Jainism, a religion practised by 4 to 5 million people, mainly in India, yoghurt is actually considered a restricted food. Because one of the major tenets is to do no harm and preserve every living creature, it is considered cruel to eat yoghurt and its billions of live and active microorganisms. The exception is yoghurt that is fermented and eaten on the same day, as the shorter incubation means fewer live bacteria have had a chance to develop. Every year, based on the Hindu lunar calendar, members of the Sikh, Jain and Hindu faiths observe a celebration of lights called Diwali. According to renowned chef Floyd Cardoz, who hailed from Mumbai, Diwali is 'Thanksgiving, Fourth of July and Christmas all rolled into one'.[1] And while sweet treats rule the day, yoghurt is a prominent dish during the five-day celebration,

Panchamrita: in Sanskrit *panch* means five and *amrut* is nectar, hence the name of the dish using five holy ingredients: milk, ghee, honey, sugar and yoghurt.

Traditional *puri bhaji* as served in a Mumbai restaurant.

including *puri bhaji*, a puffed-up, deep-fried Indian bread, made with either flour or potato and served with salad or yoghurt.

It seems that yoghurt can take its place with manna from heaven as one of the few foods that can claim such prominence in so many of the world's longest-practised religions and oldest religious scriptures.

3
Micro-management

There is a true story that sounds like the stuff of fairy tales: Francois 1, king of France, had an interesting encounter with yoghurt. The story goes something like this: once upon a time, in the mid-1500s, the French king was suffering from severe stomach issues and depression. His cadre of doctors could not figure out how to cure him. The French ambassador reached out to their ally, Sultan Suleiman the Magnificent of the Ottoman Empire. He asked him to dispatch a Jewish doctor who was known to brew fermented sheep's milk with recuperative properties. The doctor, who would only travel by foot (possibly because of restrictions regarding travel on the Sabbath), walked from southern Europe to France, with his personal flock of sheep following him. After his arrival, the doctor apparently fed the brew to the king daily, and within weeks the king was cured. It was not as good an outcome for the doctor's sheep, however, as they supposedly caught cold in Paris and did not make the trip back. Surprisingly, despite this miraculous 'cure', yoghurt did not fully catch on in France at that time.

Three hundred years later, towards the end of the nineteenth century, those microorganisms that were harnessed by Neolithic man were literally being examined with a more modern lens. Microbiologists were trying to prove Hippocrates' mantra that 'All disease begins in the gut.' To help you digest this premise, every microbe you ingest interacts with your gut (your entire digestive tract), forming colonies known as your microbiome. Much like a fingerprint, your microbiome is unique to you and can identify the country in which you were born, the last place you travelled or what you ate for lunch. It weighs 1.5 kg (3 to 4 lb), has more than 5,000 species and contains an astounding 100 trillion bacteria (gut flora or gut microbiota).

In the late 1800s to early 1900s, the microbiome was receiving much attention. Most prominent among the researchers was Professor Élie (Ilya, Ilyich) Metchnikoff, a Russian-born zoologist who studied microbes and their role in immunity, for which he won a Nobel Prize in 1908. Working in the lab at the Pasteur Institute, Metchnikoff advanced theories that ageing was a result of harmful bacteria that could colonize in your gut. He felt that by introducing yoghurt and its billions of strains of healthy bacteria into your system,

Nobel laureate Élie Metchnikoff, 1913.

your army of good bacteria will overcome the bad ones, meaning less stomach distress and, he would argue, an overall better outlook for a healthier and longer life. He further posited that high levels of lactic acid like those found in Bulgarian 'sour-milk' might be the key to a healthy gut.

Another scientist in a lab several thousand kilometres away was also tinkering with that very same premise. Bulgarian microbiologist Stamen Grigorov (Grigoroff), like Metchnikoff, hypothesized that there must be something special about lactic acid bacteria (LAB), which is prevalent in Bulgarian yoghurt. He wondered, how was it that despite their humble environment, those people raised in Bulgaria, for whom yoghurt was a mainstay of their diet, lived far longer than the general world population? Working in a lab in Switzerland, Grigorov brought with him a traditional Bulgarian clay pot known as a *rukatka*. The pot was filled with homemade

A traditional *rukatka* in the Museum of Traditional Crafts and Applied Arts, Troyan, Bulgaria.

yoghurt from his country. It was studying this sample that led Grigorov to identify the rod-like bacteria present in Bulgarian yoghurt.

That bacteria, later named, in honour of his mother country, *Lactobacillus bulgaricus*, was recently re-termed *Lactobacillus delbrueckii* subsp. *bulgaricus*. News of Grigorov's breakthrough reached Metchnikoff and cemented the latter's theories on yoghurt and longevity.

It was the confirmation of his assumptions about Bulgarian yoghurt that was the foundation of Metchnikoff's groundbreaking speech that Luba Vikhanski, author of *Immunity: How Elie Metchnikoff Changed the Course of Modern Medicine*, credits as being the turning point in yoghurt's history:

> It's rare to be able to trace a global dietary trend to a single event, but the modern yogurt industry was arguably born in the lecture hall of the Society of French Agriculture in Paris on June 8, 1904 – the day Metchnikoff delivered there a public lecture, '*La Vieillese*' (Old Age).

In that lecture, Metchnikoff went on to tout the importance of the good bacteria found in sour milk:

> This microbe is found in sour milk consumed in large amounts by the Bulgarians in a region well-known for the longevity of its inhabitants. There is therefore reason to suppose that introducing Bulgarian sour milk into the diet can reduce the harmful effect of the intestinal flora.[1]

Metchnikoff and his anti-ageing, yoghurt-eating theories became an overnight sensation. The next morning, the

Lactobacilline pills such as these were manufactured by the Paris company Le Ferment *c.* 1905–10. The package insert states that they are composed of 'pure cultures of lactic bacilli' and that they have been prepared according to the instructions of Professor Metchnikoff.

French newspaper *Le Temps* reported on the speech, exclaiming, 'Those of you, pretty ladies and brilliant gentlemen, who don't want to age or die, here's the precious recipe: eat *yaghourt*!' Vikhanski writes that the elite of Paris would wander into their local haunt to try the speciality of the house and take home what some termed their 'five o'clock yoghourt'. Pharmacies began selling the Bulgarian bacteria, even marketing it (with and without his permission) as Metchnikoff's miracle cure. The public began viewing yoghurt as a 'medicinal supplement', which prompted medical journals to weigh in. *The Lancet* suggested the public get a doctor's approval before ingesting the 'sour-milk' treatment, and the *British Medical Journal* said, 'yoghourt can be used for an indefinite time without harmful results if the dose be not too large, 1 kg a day should not customarily be exceeded.'[2]

It was not just the European press that fuelled the media frenzy and influenced buying habits. Stories about this new wonder food began to populate newspapers and magazines across the globe. A 1905 article from the *Chicago Journal* described yoghurt this way:

Curdled milk . . . prepared only on a Bulgarian recipe, is now supposed to be a remedy against growing old . . . the substance is called yoghurt . . . it is supposed to be death to all the inimical bacteria in the intestines, while those friendly microbes to which Prof. Metchnikoff pins his faith positively adore it . . . The substance looks very much like ordinary cream cheese gone bad and tastes similarly. People who wish to live to a hundred breakfast off yoghurt exclusively.

In 1905, in response to the heightened awareness of yoghurt, Metchnikoff published a brochure that detailed how it should be prepared at home. He proposed boiling the milk for a few minutes, cooling it and then introducing the bacteria. He then instructed the reader to cover it and let it stand for several hours in a warm place. The 'recipe' he provided is essentially the same process that was serendipitously discovered in 6500

German journalist Anita Joachim enjoying her bowl of skyr yoghurt, 1934.

BCE and is still in use today. Over the next several years, yoghurt continued to garner attention, but not all of it was positive. Some experts, such as Dr Harvey Wiley, an American chemist who became the first commissioner of the Food and Drug Administration (FDA), ridiculed Metchnikoff's ideas of a single food being the elixir of life and cast aspersions on the connection between sour milk and longevity. In the middle of the first decade of the 1900s, an article appeared in the American magazine *Medical News* that noted that 'one would be tempted to suspect that he (Metchnikoff) amuses himself by practicing on the gullibility of the public.' Metchnikoff himself tried to tone down the claims by saying, 'I have never in any of my publications on the subject asserted that curdled milk is able to prolong life.' At this same time, mysticism became a fascination in Europe. In response to this trend, in 1908 Metchnikoff published his pre-eminent work *Études optimistes*, which English translators expanded as *The Prolongation of Life: Optimistic Studies*. In it, he espoused numerous theories and concepts from social to medical, and it became his defining work.

Throughout the decade following Metchnikoff's discoveries there were many humorous observations on the yoghurt trend, with journalists not knowing exactly how to report on the phenomenon. One such article published in April 1912 in the *Winnipeg Tribune* said of the number of centenarians in Bulgaria, 'They live until their neighbors are tired of seeing them hanging around.' Another published in the *Vancouver Daily World* from 1913 suggests Metchnikoff's microbes will allow you to 'compete with your daughters in beauty, with your sons in strength.'

In an interesting aside, Metchnikoff's discoveries caught the attention of several Russian luminaries: Lenin, Tolstoy and the Russian ex-pat Chaim Weizmann, who became the

Hector Moloch's caricature of Professor Metchnikoff, satirizing his theory of longevity, published in *Chanteclair*, June 1908.

first president of Israel. At the time, Lenin was a struggling revolutionary who crossed paths with Metchnikoff. Wanting to recruit Metchnikoff for the cause, Lenin commented to Weizmann, 'Every time I meet our friend Ilya Metchnikoff, I thank him for his yoghurt and reproach him for staying away from the social issues of mankind.'[3] In a separate interaction, Metchnikoff and the writer Tolstoy were said to be on opposite sides about most things, but it was known that the one thing they agreed on was yoghurt.

One devoted disciple of Metchnikoff was Dr John Harvey Kellogg. Kellogg, credited with establishing cereal as the breakfast of choice, was considered unconventional in his medical practices, which were evident at his holistic sanatorium in Battle Creek, Michigan. He visited Metchnikoff at the Pasteur lab and upon returning from a visit with yoghurt cultures in hand, he prescribed it as treatment, delivering it in part through eating, and without being too graphic, administered the balance as an enema. In his book *Autointoxication* (1919), he wrote that Metchnikoff had 'placed the whole world under obligation to him in his discovery that the flora of the human intestine needs changing'.[4]

Metchnikoff and Grigorov were not the only scientists busily identifying bacterial strains associated with yoghurt. The body of work by microbiologists in isolating, experimenting and naming bacteria that led to advancements in yoghurt production included many other impressive notables. Among them was the British surgeon Dr Joseph Lister, who, in the late 1800s, was best known for his work in antiseptic techniques. What some don't know is that he too studied lactic acid bacteria and their role in fermenting milk and aiding in gut health. His work was expanded by the Danish chemist Sigurd Orla-Jensen, who, in 1919, published the results of a ten-year study in *Mémoires de l'Academie Royale des*

Sciences et des Lettres de Danemark, Copenhague, in which he identified *Streptococcus thermophilus* (heat-loving bacteria). In later work, Orla-Jensen reported on the bacteria that work symbiotically in yoghurt. The bacterium he identified is the partner to LAB in production of all commercial yoghurt in the United Sates and most of the world. A paediatrician named Ernst Moro is credited with isolating *Lactobacillus acidophilus*, a powerful probiotic. In the same lab as Metchnikoff, the French paediatrician Dr Henri Tissier focused his research on children suffering from stomach issues. He noticed they had a low number of 'bifid' bacteria, while healthy children had a greater concentration. Tissier suggested that children's microbiomes could be restored by eating the good bacteria that is used to ferment yoghurt. It was Tissier's discovery that led to *Bifidobacteria* often being added to yoghurt along with *Lactobacillus acidophilus* to boost probiotic efficacy.

Hippocrates would have been proud of the intense new scrutiny the gut was receiving and the impact his ancient theory had on modern science. It led to yoghurt's next iteration as a mainstream food in a health-conscious society.

4
Yoghurt Goes to Market

In the early twentieth century the world was continuing to respond and react to the investigations into yoghurt's benefits. One of the voices that emerged was that of Isaac Carasso, who, like so many others, was influenced by Metchnikoff and saw the medicinal benefits of yoghurt. In 1912 Carasso, a Sephardic Jew, moved from Greece back to his family's birthplace of Spain. He took with him a love for yoghurt and opened a small plant in Barcelona intending to produce and sell yoghurt to pharmacies throughout the country. It was seven years later, in 1919, that Carasso officially ushered in the commercial age of yoghurt. He named his company Danone (Catalan for 'little Daniel'), in honour of his son Daniel.

In her book *Immunity*, Vikhanski quotes Daniel Carasso, who was commenting on the yoghurt giant's humble beginnings: 'We used tinned-copper vats to heat the milk and stirred it by hand with wooden paddles . . . we added the yogurt culture with a pipette, one jar at a time. We used a culture strain supplied by the Pasteur Institute.'[1] Daniel went on to study bacteriology at the Institute and in 1929 established the Société Parisienne du Yoghourt in Paris. In 1941 Daniel fled the Nazis and emigrated to the United States. There he established a presence in the Bronx, New York, Americanized the product name to Dannon and, together with Juan Metzger, brought yoghurt to a wide market. (It is worth noting that the multinational yoghurt corporation currently based in France is known as Danone, while the product in the U.S. is called Dannon.)

In 1942 Metzger tried to mount a campaign to market yoghurt as a meat substitute, a concept that didn't exactly catch on. However, he did have an 'aha' moment in 1947, when the company introduced yoghurt with fruit at the bottom of the cup, strawberry being the first flavour. That took yoghurt from being seen solely as health food to a delightfully sweet concoction that was suitable for breakfast, lunch, dinner or even dessert. At the urging of Metzger, their product stayed ahead of the curve by investing in aggressive advertising. In 1973 Danone launched its iconic advertising campaign featuring healthy, aged, active Soviet Georgian peasants eating yoghurt. In one such advert, the narrator observed,

At the outset, yoghurt was packaged in glass bottles, as seen in this early 1940s Dannon advertisement in the U.S.

Photo from Danone's iconic *In Soviet Georgia* (also called *Old People in Russia*) advertising campaign in the U.S. depicting ageing yoghurt lovers, 1973.

In Soviet Georgia, there are two curious things about the people. A large part of their diet is yogurt. And a large number of them live past a hundred. We're not saying that Dannon yogurt will help you live longer, but Dannon low fat yogurt is a wholesome natural food rich in nutrition.[2]

Danone continued to innovate and educate and might be considered one of the first yoghurt companies to seize the concept of yoghurt being a functional food. In the mid-1990s, it launched Actimel, a probiotic-rich product, which within three years of its release grew the UK probiotic market from £3 million to £62 million. However, in complete contrast with and – some might say – to the detriment of yoghurt, in 1992 they debuted sprinkles as an add-in. The company eventually moved back to France, where, in 2005, Pepsi launched a takeover bid. It was quickly squashed by the government, and it appeared the entire country was protecting Danone from an American takeover. The *New York Times* reported that the French called Danone a 'national icon', and Prime Minister de Villepin labelled it 'an industrial treasure'. Today, Danone is the largest distributor of yoghurt worldwide, reaching nearly every market on the globe.

While Carasso left Greece to launch his yoghurt empire, another family business was staking a claim in that part of the world for theirs. Fage (pronounced 'Fah-yeh', which is Greek for 'to eat') was the first branded yoghurt in Greece. The Filippou family opened their shop in Athens back in 1926, making *straggisto* yoghurt in the Greek style – that is, straining several times to release most of the whey. The result is a tart and oh-so-thick product that takes 1.8 kg (4 lb) of milk to make 450 g (1 lb) of yoghurt. After the Filippou family established their company's presence in Greece as the number-one yoghurt brand, they expanded the company into the European market. But their big breakthrough came when Kostas Mastoras, the owner of a Greek food market in Queens, New York, tasted the yoghurt on a purchasing trip to Athens. He was so enamoured of the product that he risked a customs violation and took containers back home with him. The yoghurt was a huge hit, and he began distributing Greek yoghurt throughout New York, making it the first Greek yoghurt introduced to the United States.

But the Carassos and the Filippous were not the only families banking on yoghurt being the next big thing; another family-owned business was blazing their own yoghurt legacy. The Colombosians, who hailed from Armenia, brought with them to Massachusetts a rich history of yoghurt-making. Their yoghurt business, run out of their garage, was literally a by-product of their milk business, as they used their leftover milk to produce *matzoon*, as Armenians call yoghurt. They shortened their name on their yoghurt labels to Colombo, making it easier to pronounce, and on the eve of America's Great Depression peddled the yoghurt via horse-drawn carriages. As Joel Denker explains in his book *The World on a Plate* (2003), their customers were immigrants from Middle Eastern and Greek backgrounds who craved the yoghurt they used to make daily and now had no time to prepare. Just as Danone had, the Colombosians also began sweetening their yoghurt, and in the mid-1960s added fruit to the bottom of their cups to make the taste more palatable to Americans. According to Bob Colombosian, one of the founder's sons, he was now hopeful that people would no longer 'spit it out when they took a bite'. The family retained ownership through the 1970s, when they were bought out by General Mills. Quite a long and prestigious run for a family business that started in a garage.

A relative newcomer to the commercialization of yoghurt was Yoplait, a French concern that was established in 1965, when a group of dairy farmers from six dairy co-ops in France formed the company. Their name derives from the combination of two of the co-ops, Yola and Coplait, and the six-leaf logo is a homage to the company's bucolic beginnings. In 1981 Yoplait was making a name for itself in North America, first on the West Coast, but soon after throughout the United States. In talking about this chic new brand, articles circulated in every major newspaper across the u.s. spread their tag line, 'get a little taste of French culture'. Yoplait broke with its competitors when it began using a 170-gram (6 oz) plastic cup, rather than the 225-gram (8 oz) jar that was the norm, their food scientists citing the new dimensions as the perfect portion and conveyance.

Using freeze-dried active cultures flown in from France and processed in Michigan, their strains were less acidic and therefore had a sweeter flavour. What differentiated them most was the style of yoghurt they prepared. They moved away from set style, also known as 'sundae style', in which the fruit is on the bottom of the cup and the yoghurt is a bit thicker, to a Swiss style, in which the fruit is blended in. The resulting texture is creamier and the consistency lighter, almost like a chiffon parfait. Other manufacturers followed suit, offering Swiss style as well as fruit on the bottom. If imitation is the sincerest form of flattery, Yoplait must have been blushing. Headlines across America proclaimed 'Yogurt war' as Yoplait and Dannon went head-to-head in California. One stock boy from a market in Encino, California, who observed a yoghurt-buying frenzy, was quoted in a 1980 *Los Angeles Times* article as saying: 'People panic during a crisis.

Yoplait reinvented the yoghurt container with their recognizable tapered plastic cup.

Earthquakes, threat of war, they go crazy and stock up on food . . . but for yogurt, I just don't understand it.'[3]

At almost the same time that Yoplait was establishing their brand in France, Nestlé introduced Ski, a Swiss-style yoghurt, to the UK. Ski was a breakthrough product for the UK market, as it included real fruit pieces and sweetness from added sugar. These little pots, according to Stephen Logue, senior product manager of Ski at that time, 'delivered an organoleptic [those characteristics that interpret mouthfeel, taste and texture] treat not so far experienced by British consumers.'[4]

In 1972 Ski sold an astounding 150 million pots and captured a 42 per cent market share. Even Harrods, Fortnum & Mason and Selfridges carried the product before major grocers began selling it in their dairy aisles. Ski's presence was soon challenged by St Ivel's Prize and Unilever's Cool Country. None of these brands is considered the top seller in the UK today, but they were the trailblazers for those yet to come. Müller was one of the next generations of yoghurt companies to appeal to the UK consumer. Started by Theobald Müller in a small Bavarian town in Germany, where it is the largest private dairy, it began distributing to the UK in 1987 and has held the top position ever since. The UK seemed to be a market ripe for innovative products: in the late 1990s, Yakult probiotic drinks and then Danone's Actimel established functional foods as a real thing for British consumers interested in probiotics and health food.

No conversation on yoghurt influencers would be complete without discussing the one that most recently disrupted the entire field, Turkish-Kurdish born Hamdi Ulukaya. In 2005 he founded Chobani, a company that started the Greek yoghurt craze in America. Ulukaya's secret was tapping into the consumer's desire for a protein-rich yoghurt with a

Chobani, the great yoghurt disrupter of the 21st century.

low-fat profile. In less than five years, the upstate New York company ranked number one in sales and increased Greek yoghurt's market share from 1 per cent in 2007 to more than 50 per cent in 2013.

Much like the herdsmen in his home region so many years before, Hamdi's fortune could be called serendipitous. He saw an advert for a yoghurt factory in upstate New York, located near a plant where he was producing his father's coveted feta cheese. He didn't set out to make Greek yoghurt; he just happened upon the opportunity and seized it. He enlisted the help of a yoghurt master from his homeland and after tinkering with a combination of strains, developed their signature Greek yoghurt. Ulukaya used unconventional and creative business practice to bring his yoghurt to market, including giving grocers free yoghurt in lieu of the customary stocking fee. He brought his yoghurt to the masses via his Cho-mobile, which dispensed free samples, and he used social media to create incredible buzz. It wasn't long before Chobani became a household name and supplanted Fage in sales in the u.s. The Greek yoghurt wars were officially on, and the dairy aisle would never be the same. Chobani and Fage faced off in a battle to see who could claim the use of the word 'Greek' in connection with their yoghurt. Fage won a victory of sorts, as they can market their yoghurt in Britain as 'authentic Greek yoghurt', which they felt sounded more genuine, whereas Chobani's needs to be labelled 'strained', which might sound more processed. However, in the u.s., Chobani held on to the term 'Greek'. The loser in all this was Greece, who, in a big misstep, did not trademark the term.

For the u.s. market, it is interesting how many companies produce their yoghurt in New York, where more Greek yoghurt is produced than even in Greece. The New York state of mind is so rooted in yoghurt that in 2014 Governor Andrew Cuomo designated yoghurt as the official New York state snack. In what some called a diplomatic nightmare, that same year the Russian government blocked a shipment of 5,000 containers of New York's own Chobani yoghurt from reaching the United States Winter Olympic team in Sochi.

Playing by the Rules

Entering the twenty-first century, you now had a product that after close to 10,000 years was a bona fide commercial success, and with that came manufacturing facilities to meet the demand. Processing yoghurt is pretty standard, and while small batch or artisanal brands might tweak the preparation, most manufacturers follow the same process as was described by Metchnikoff in his 1905 brochure. Compare that century-old recipe to what is standard today and you will see very little difference. The language has evolved, and the facilities are sophisticated, but all commercial milk-based yoghurt essentially goes through the same steps. It all starts with the milk, whether it be whole, low fat or non-fat (skimmed). Non-fat dried milk or whey powder can be added to contribute to the milk solids and create more structure, and to bump the milk fat, cream is sometimes incorporated. Pasteurization and homogenization of the milk is followed by a period of cooling down prior to the inoculation of the starter culture to the milk. To be called yoghurt in the U.S., it must contain the hard-to-pronounce and even-harder-to-spell *Streptococcus thermophilus* and *Lactobacillus bulgaricus* (hereafter known as STLB). Like peanut butter and jam, these two bacteria complement each other.

For set-style yoghurt, fruit is added to the cup at this stage, and the yoghurt is placed on top of the fruit base before fermentation. For Swiss style, the fruit is added at the end. For all preparations, incubation takes anywhere from four to seven hours at a temperature that hovers between 40°C (105°F) and 46°C (115°F). Too high a temperature and the starter cultures are killed, too low and they cannot sustain growth. After that time, the correct pH level of 4.6 is reached, and you have yoghurt. If a second pasteurization takes place, or to get additional health benefits, other strains of probiotic bacteria can be added. The final step is date stamping the containers. Fermentation does extend yoghurt's shelf life, but it should be enjoyed within 7 to 21 days after purchase. Refrigerated drinkable yoghurt has a slightly shorter window, and ambient (non-chilled) yoghurt a much longer one. Once yoghurt is opened, its nutritional value diminishes, so to get your best probiotic bang for your buck, eat, enjoy and repeat.

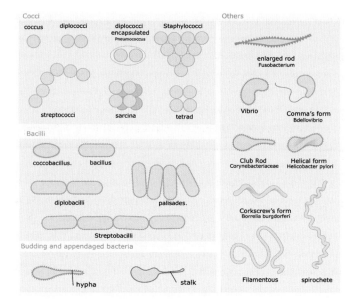

Bacteria take many shapes: in yoghurt *Lactobacillus bulgaricus* represents the rod-like bacteria, while *Streptococcus thermophilus* appears spherical.

However, if this standard production were the same for every single unit of yoghurt produced, then what would differentiate yoghurt A from yoghurt B? In speaking with Michael Neuwirth, senior director of external communications for Danone North America, he has explained, 'making yoghurt is part science and part art.' Within STLB, there is a plethora of strains, each carrying its own nuance to make the taste and texture of the yoghurt unique. Producers strive to create proprietary products with signature strains to achieve the perfect balance. With yoghurt, there are infinite combinations. For example, housed outside of Paris, Danone has what is called a 'library' of over three hundred living strains that are subtypes of STLB. Food scientists play with different blends of these strains to achieve a singular balance of discernible characteristics. So, while all yoghurts do go through the same process, there is a world of combinations to create the variety of options we enjoy today.

Regulation always follows production, in this case by establishing the necessary rules to which all commercially produced yoghurts would have to adhere. In the United States, the FDA oversees those standards. In Title 21, Chapter 1, Subchapter B Part 131.200 in the FDA Code of Federal Regulations you will find the laws governing what is and is not yoghurt and what can and cannot be included in its production. To make quick work of a very long code, yoghurt must contain STLB. All yoghurt must be at least 8.25 per cent milk solids. Full-fat yoghurt must contain no less than 3.25 per cent milk fat, low-fat yoghurt no more than 2 per cent milk fat and non-fat yoghurt less than 0.5 per cent milk fat. Yoghurt must not have an acidity level less than 0.9 per cent expressed as lactic acid. Vitamins can be added, as can additional sweeteners, food additives, flavour enhancers, colour additives and stabilizers such as pectin, gelatin or xanthan gum. Labelling must include all these ingredients as well as terms such as 'homogenized' and 'heat treated after culturing'. The label must additionally represent which microorganisms are present and in what amount. This notation, generally seen as Colony Forming Units (CFUs), helps the consumer know how much live and active bacteria are truly present. In the U.S., a seal issued by the International Dairy Foods Association called the 'Live and Active Cultures Seal' (LAC) is a visual assurance on a label that the product contains significant live and active cultures. In the absence of the seal, look for a notation such as 10^6, which indicates CFUs of 100 million cultures per gram. Other bacterial cultures, such as *Lactobacillus acidophilus*, *Lactobacillus* subsp. *casei* and *Bifido-bacteria* may be added to boost the probiotic content. All of this information can be found on the label, so be sure to take your reading glasses next time you shop for yoghurt.

In an effort to have an international consensus with regard to food standards and safe practice, as well as to ensure fair trade, there is an international body known as the Codex Alimentarius. This arm of the World Health Organization (WHO) and Food and Agriculture Organizations of the United Nations has 189 member countries including the U.S., the UK and some nations in the EU, along with most industrialized countries. Codex standards are voluntary, and it is left up to each country as to how the codes are interpreted, regulated and enforced. One of the foods the Codex addresses is yoghurt, and it carries a set of rules (Codex Stan 243-2003) that determine what does and does not constitute yoghurt. The basic guidelines conform to what the FDA established, with distinguishing features varying country by country. Take Canada, for instance, where there is no federal standard, and the National Dairy Code is relied upon. The code essentially agrees with the Codex in that, in order to be called yoghurt, our two famous bacteria must be present, but little else is regulated. In the UK, yoghurt can still qualify even if only one of the two traditional bacteria is used, and in places such as Japan and Finland, there are no set guidelines or compositional regulations for any milk products. But, of course, as one would expect (and hope), Bulgaria has precise requirements, as expressed in their Dairy Products Ordinance, and makes three differentiations. 'Sour milk' is what we would term traditional Bulgarian yoghurt, and it must be fermented with STLB. Milk with STLB as well as additional lactic acid can be called yoghurt, and products that have STLB and lactic acid, but not enough microflora to fulfil their requirement, would be called 'lactic acid products'.

In the case of regulating fermented drinks such as milk with acidophilus, *kefir* and *kumys*, on which water is added, at least 40 per cent of the product must be fermented milk for the produce to be labelled as a fermented product. The European Commission ruled in 2015 that a plant-based yoghurt cannot be called 'yoghurt', as they feel it leads to consumer confusion. The FDA is currently tackling that issue. Additionally, health claims by yoghurt producers are treated differently from country to country. In the United States, the FDA very tightly regulates health claims. There are only a handful of allowable ones in the U.S., so to say yoghurt controls obesity would not be allowed; however, you can say that it helps keep weight in check. In 2012 the European Food Safety Authority ruled that no health claims regarding probiotics and yoghurt would be permitted, denying 74 petitions from companies who had the science to back their claim. In what seems like a funny addition to the Codex, 'yoghurt may be spelled as appropriate in the country of retail sale', hence the 'h' throughout this book, no 'h' in the U.S. and, in some places, the addition of 'ou'. It is interesting to note that in an effort to modernize and conventionalize the spelling, many countries are moving towards dropping the 'h', while traditionalists prefer to keep it. It would seem that the rules regulating yoghurt will be evolving for some time.

5
Culture Shock

Visit any dairy or frozen food aisle, and a dizzying array of yoghurt options is there to greet you. The market has moved dramatically from offering limited options such as set-style fruit-on-the-bottom yoghurt, stirred Swiss-style blended yoghurt or simply plain yoghurt. This chapter is here to serve as a cheat sheet to help you wade through the aisle, when you are knee-deep in yoghurt choices.

The most important ingredient when choosing any type of yoghurt is the presence of live and active cultures. All yoghurts commercially produced must list this clearly on their label. As we know, not all yoghurts are created equal: some might contain additional probiotics and vitamins or unwanted additives and too much sugar. When comparing labels, size matters, so be sure you are looking at comparable containers, as single-serving yoghurts are packaged most commonly in a 150 g (5.3 oz) container but can also be found in 170 g (6 oz) and 225 g (8 oz) sizes. When reading the label, the first ingredient listed is the most prominent in the product, so for dairy yoghurt, be sure cultured milk is the first and for plant-based, look for that milk substitute to be listed at the top. Most yoghurts will also call out the total fat (both saturated and non-saturated), cholesterol, sodium, potassium, total carbohydrate, dietary fibre, sugars and protein levels. What is

The yoghurt aisle is longer than any other in this New York supermarket.

not in the container is often more important than what is, so look for labelling that identifies if the product is free of artificial flavours or preservatives, or additional fillers or starches, thickeners or sugars. With the trend towards clean labelling, which means having the fewest ingredients in a product, manufacturers are taking note and trying to subtract rather than add.

When Greek yoghurt burst onto the scene, it was a game changer. What made this 'new' product so unique and appealing was that it had a naturally tart taste and thick texture and was touted as being a healthier alternative to traditional yoghurt. The public ate it up. Not only did Greek yoghurt producers decide to package their yoghurt in shorter, wider containers, to differentiate them from traditional yoghurts, but they added wording on their labels to call out the protein content. With about 17 g (½ oz) of protein per serving (about the same as 2 to 3 oz of lean meat) as compared to 9 g (⅓ oz) in regular yoghurt, Greek yoghurt is a protein powerhouse. By draining

Close-up of whey being released during the straining process.

the whey, the product has 50 per cent fewer carbohydrates and fewer milk sugars.

If you are watching your sodium, Greek yoghurt is the winner in that category, with about half the sodium found in regular yoghurt. In addition to its other pluses, Greek yoghurt has great interchangeability in recipes. It's a terrific substitute for sour cream when making a savoury dip, does not curdle when slowly heated, can stand in for mayo in dishes like egg or potato salad, and makes a good substitute for traditional fats in baked goods. When a recipe calls for yoghurt, you'll have a richer finish if you use Greek instead of regular. However, it's not all sunny news for Greek yoghurt. It does contain more fat than regular yoghurt and has less potassium and calcium. Beware of those imposter products that achieve Greek yoghurt's consistency by adding thickeners like corn starch or milk protein concentrate (MPC).

Greek yoghurt is not the only good choice when browsing the dairy case, as there are some terrific BFFs (Best Fermented Friends) keeping it company. Now available in markets across the globe is Icelandic-style yoghurt, which might be the closest to Greek due to its straining process and protein punch, but with a silkier finish and less fat. *Skyr* (pronounced skeer), is a traditional Nordic yoghurt dating back to the days of the Vikings. The Norse learned how to manipulate bacterial strains, ferment skimmed milk and prolong milk's viability. After all, Viking sea voyages could be quite lengthy. In the U.S., Icelandic yoghurt is realizing meteoric sales and aspires to disrupt the market as Greek yoghurt did.

Icelandic-style skyr is taking up a lot of space in the yoghurt aisle.

If it's a luxuriously fatty mouthfeel you're craving, you can say you're following doctor's orders and eat full-fat yoghurt or those that have tripled down on cream. Research released in 2018 went viral as a study of nearly 3,000 U.S. adults was published regarding the relationship between high-fat dairy and CVD (coronary vascular disease). They noted that some of the properties in the higher-fat varieties might be protective of our heart health, help boost metabolism and reduce obesity by up to 8 per cent.[1]

Products such as Peak Yogurt are capitalizing on that premise and following the keto diet, which shuns carbs and favours high fat. In speaking to Evan Sims, founder of Peak Yogurt, he made a simple case for his high-fat food, saying, 'keto has blown up as a movement . . . milk fat is the best part of dairy, [it] has all the critical fat-soluble nutrients.' Siggi Hilmarsson, the founder of one of the best-known Icelandic yoghurts, Siggi's, is a fan of their triple-cream product. As a child, he remembers eating yoghurt with a healthy pouring of cream on top; Siggi's version, called *rjoma*, is a homage to one of his favourite childhood memories.

Australian yoghurt is another entry that has its own proprietary taste and texture. Generally regarded as an indulgent yoghurt, it is full fat and proud of it. Two brands that are leaders in this category are Noosa and Wallaby, and both feature a creamy texture with more protein than traditional yoghurt, but less than Icelandic or Greek. Some have credited Australian yoghurt with bringing decadence back to the dairy case and pushing aside yoghurt's persona as a diet food. Australian yoghurt makes a great choice as a dessert, with its rich flavour and luscious texture, and is seeing rapid growth.

Refusing to be ignored is the unapologetically adorable glass pot of French-style yoghurt. Its flirtatious adornments include chequered cloth lids or delicate bows. It speaks

French, of course, and carries with it names like 'Oui by Yoplait'. These yoghurts are often cultured right in the jars that are found in your dairy case, so it is unstrained and generally has more sugar than most other styles. But if you want an authentic French experience, you might want to give it a try.

Moooove over

Where you live can ultimately determine the milk source your yoghurt is made from, as you will discover a variety of alternatives to traditional cow's milk. One entry, although potentially hard to find – unless you are a Bedouin – is camel's milk. This milk is super rich in iron and vitamin C and is lower in total and saturated fat, with a higher quantity of proteins, than cow's milk. Easier to obtain is yoghurt made from buffalo milk. The product is as thick as Greek yoghurt, with less tang or need for straining. Ithaca Milk, a company based in New York State, have a yoghurt made with water buffalo milk. The company calls it 'the most natural yogurt' they can make. 'It is higher in protein and lower in saturated fat than cow's milk . . . naturally making a thick Greek-like yogurt without having to strain . . . The result is zero waste, and 100% natural, thick yogurt, that is smooth and not sour with lower acidity than Greek yogurt.'[2] Back in 2013, Mintel (a global market research firm) noted only two companies producing water buffalo yoghurt. As of 2017 there were eleven, with Chile, Romania and Turkey leading the pack in production. Quebec is now the home to a herd of water buffalo, brought to North America via the Lazio region of Italy. The yoghurt produced from these animals has the same characteristic creamy and rich flavour and texture that makes buffalo mozzarella such a delicacy. Consumers in India and parts of Asia already accept

Yoghurt made from water buffalo milk has a distinct creaminess similar to burrata made from the same milk source.

this replacement for bovine milk and have made it one of the most popular alternatives.

If water buffalo produce is not your thing, maybe goat's milk is. With its lemony, 'goaty', pungent flavour, it is easy to digest and is a popular choice for those allergic to cow's milk. It is low in fat and rich in calcium, potassium and magnesium; has a tonne of vitamin A; and contains loads of those healthy short- and medium-chain fatty acids. Its protein is more easily digested than cow's milk, but it tends to be runny, so additives are often needed to give it structure.

If you want to eat yoghurt with a rich, buttery taste, then you might seek out sheep's milk, which is higher in fat than cow's milk – the good fat with all its benefits. It has more CLA (conjugated linoleic acid – purported to help with weight loss and to contain cancer-fighting agents) than cow's or goat's milk, and has more calcium, iron and vitamin B12 than cow's milk. Compared to goat's milk, it contains more folic acid and more iron. Manufacturers such as Old Chatham and Bellwether are making inroads in America, but there are small-batch artisanal farms sharing their bovine goodness with you locally, such as Pecora in Australia and Woodlands in the UK. France is leading the rest of the world in alternatives to cow's milk, with goat's milk and sheep's milk products. Nestlé Lactalis is betting their sheep's milk yoghurt, Lou Pérac, will resonate with French consumers. Find a region where sheep are ever present, and you are sure to find locally sourced sheep's milk yoghurt.

Yoghurt's newest stars are the plant-based varieties, which have grown at a rate of 55 per cent per year, with sales expected

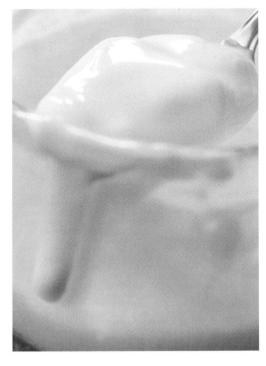

Goat's milk yoghurt has a distinctive tangy flavour and a slightly runnier consistency than cow's milk.

to top U.S.$12 billion dollars in the next decade. Market Watch, published by Dow Jones, Inc., reported in February 2020 that they expect to see this segment of the yoghurt market achieve an astounding CAGR (compound annual growth rate) of 13 per cent by 2025. Many consumers, especially millennials, are moving towards vegan (no animal-derived products), flexitarian (a less strict form of vegetarianism) and 'lessitarian' (similar to flexitarianism, with the mantra of less is more) diets. Millennials speak loudly with their wallets, especially a subgroup labelled 'millennial mums', who work primarily outside the home and are focused on foods that are fast, nutritious and healthy for their kids. Joining the trend are seniors, who are looking for non-dairy options with probiotic benefits, bone-density-building blocks and low-calorie intake. Together,

Sheep roam the fields of Blackberry Farm, Tennessee, where their milk is used to make the farm's signature sweet yoghurt.

these disparate generations are finding common ground in the dairy aisle and changing the yoghurt landscape.

Plant-based and dairy-free yoghurts are just what they sound like: they are derived from plants, nuts, legumes, seeds and grains and contain all the nutrients found in their base source without any dairy whatsoever. Soy was the first plant-based yoghurt to emerge and was embraced for good reason. Its properties have particular success in carbohydrate digestion, so you experience fewer blood sugar spikes after eating it. As a complete protein, soy contains all nine essential amino acids, so for those who are avoiding dairy, it's a great choice. It has properties that have been shown to aid with reducing harmful low-density lipoproteins (LDL), considered bad cholesterol, while boosting beneficial high-density lipoproteins (HDL), the good cholesterol. Soy, which mimics oestrogen in the body, has been controversial for some who are concerned with risks associated with oestrogen and breast cancer. The jury is out, and a substantial amount of research is being conducted to fully explore those links.

Nut 'milk' yoghurts like almond, coconut and cashew milk are supplanting soy as the number one choice. Nut-based yoghurts are made by grinding nuts and mixing them with water, and then fermenting them with bacteria, so they have all the benefits that they have in their original form. Almonds currently account for half of plant-based yoghurt sales, having the definite edge in terms of fibre. Fibre is a prebiotic that feeds the probiotics, so this is a compelling plus. Almond yoghurt includes heart-healthy fats, a good amount of hunger-satiating protein, vitamin E, manganese and magnesium, with small amounts of vitamin B12 and phosphorous. This combination of nutrients shows almond yoghurt to be a good choice for those tackling cholesterol, blood pressure and weight issues. It edges out cashew yoghurt in many of these

The perfect non-dairy snack: almond yoghurt topped with coconut, walnuts and a drizzle of honey.

attributes, except that cashew yoghurt is rich in iron and zinc, which has been termed by some as 'brainpower boosters'. Of all the plant-based options, coconut yoghurt, with its distinct-ively 'coconutty' sweet flavour, has seen a soaring rise in sales, up 20 per cent in 2016, and that's following a 40 per cent increase the year before. It is made from pressing the white flesh of coconut and mixing it with water. It is rich in coconut fat, which enjoyed the spotlight for some time because it was considered a healthy medium-chain fat, credited with boosting good HDL cholesterol and lowering bad LDL, while promoting weight loss. However, what it gains in good fat it lacks in the protein department.

The inherent challenges for plant-based yoghurts surround their taste, texture and nutritional values, and the additives that are needed to boost all three. Nicki Briggs, chief marketing officer at Lavva non-dairy yoghurt, explained to online food source *Food Navigator*, 'Essentially, people are taking plant-based ingredients and then adding a bunch of sugar, gums and stabilizers to make products edible.'[3] Lavva, of course, points out that that's not their method, but it is the norm. Plant-based yoghurt is often supplemented with added calcium and vitamin D to make up for its shortfall, and as a spokesperson for the Academy of Nutrition and Dietetics noted, the bioavailability (the amount of calcium that's actually

Coconut milk yoghurt is just one of the popular plant-based yoghurt varieties, shown here with pomegranate, banana chips and chia seeds and presented in hollowed-out coconut shells.

absorbed) cannot compete with cow's milk. Additionally, plant-based yoghurts have to jump the sugar hurdle. Sugar is almost always added and even sugars labelled as natural, such as agave or honey, are not metabolized the same as naturally occurring sugars. Nutritionist Rachel Fine cautions to avoid artificial sweeteners, even those naturally derived like Stevia, and advises you stick with natural products that have a longer track record, saying that cane sugar has a lot more years behind it. And last, but not least, to create the proper texture, plant-based yoghurts often contain added emulsifiers and stabilizers such as guar gum and pectin – and while both are naturally occurring, so is plutonium, and you wouldn't want to ingest that. Most plant-based yoghurts are not truly as clean-labelled as dairy-based yoghurts; however, they do have benefits that often mitigate what they lack. For Fine, they 'get a B' in her book. Stressing that if you can tolerate dairy, 'stick with standard yogurt'. However, major producers are jumping on this fast-moving trend and banking on plant-based yoghurts to continue to disrupt the industry, as Greek yoghurt did a decade ago. The numbers don't lie: vegan yoghurt sales increased by 30,000 tonnes in 2018, as more and more people shift away from animal-based foods, and are expected to top 7.4 billion globally by 2027.[4]

Another trend influencing what you find in your dairy case is the need for provenance and locally sourced products. In what some are terming 'pasture to plate', yoghurt buyers want to know the history behind the product they are buying and fully utilize what nature gives us. They are trying to reduce their carbon footprints, looking for sustainable ingredients and creating as little waste as possible. Yoghurt meets the four criteria necessary to be considered a sustainable food as it is environmentally friendly, high in nutrient value, affordable and culturally acceptable.

There are a plethora of children's yoghurt products. Read the labels to make the best choices.

The war on sugar is officially being waged, and the impact is being felt especially in the children's yoghurt category. For years, cute and cuddly creatures have masqueraded as health food and have influenced parents' buying habits. Recent studies point to the extremely high levels of sugar found in all yoghurt and the efforts by manufacturers to market those sugary treats directly to children. In the UK, a 'Save the Kids from Sugar' campaign took hold, and organizations from the World Health Organization to the American Academy of Pediatrics all warn of too much sugar consumption by children. According to a piece posted in February 2019 on Mintel.com, Amrin Walji, a senior innovation analyst in the food industry, noted, 'the UK market is looking to cut sugar consumption by 20 per cent by 2020'. Similar goals are being expressed across the globe, as seen in Germany, where Nur yoghurt (German for 'only') is 75 per cent organic yoghurt and 25 per cent organic fruit – nothing else. In response, both Chobani and Danone North America launched new products in 2018 specifically addressing these concerns. It has been quantified that parents are willing to spend up to 50 per cent more for yoghurt products – from 'squeezables' to yoghurt melts for babies – that are free from preservatives and additives, with reduced sugar. This is incentivizing producers to take appropriate action.

Many Are Cold, but Few Are Frozen

Move over a few aisles in your market, and you are likely to need a sweater and a handbook to peruse the multitude of choices in the frozen yoghurt section. This sweet confection debuted in the United States at a time when many consumers were becoming health conscious, and the idea of eating frozen yoghurt was very appealing. However, it was not instant infatuation. The masses reported the tart taste was off-putting, some claiming that it tasted too much like yoghurt. However, players in the field such as Danone and HP Hood LLC began adding fruit and flavours to make it more palatable. You might recall 'Danny' Danone's entry into the field with its rich chocolate coating or Hood's 'frogurt' that mimicked ice cream's taste and texture.

Much like ice cream, frozen yoghurt is made by pumping air into the mixture to amplify volume, while water is added to create the ice crystals that we associate with frozen yoghurt. It would be a hard call to say frozen yoghurt is health food, as the proprietary bacteria make up only 1 per cent of its ingredients, with milk, milk products, sugar, stabilizers and emulsifiers accounting for the lion's share. Depending on the milk base, frozen yoghurt can have as little as 0.5 per cent milk fat and as much as 6 per cent. It is the fat that lends the mouthfeel and creaminess to the yoghurt base. There are several types of sugar that can be added: cane sugar, corn syrup and even beet sugar, as well as sugar substitutes. These not only add sweetness but create body and consistency. Stabilizers to prevent extensive crystallization and excessive melting are added, as are emulsifiers, both in negligible quantities. Frozen yoghurt can contain egg solids, salt, protein derivatives

Like refrigerated yoghurt, frozen yoghurt takes well to creative combinations of fresh fruits, as well as savoury add-ins.

Frozen yoghurt for four-legged friends.

and flavour enhancers such as fruit extracts, chocolate, nuts and even spices such as chai and ginger. If you are watching calories or avoiding certain ingredients, frozen yoghurt can be a nice alternative to ice cream. Take note, because frozen yoghurt is not subject to the same scrutiny regarding its ingredients and labelling as fresh yoghurt – indulge for the taste and not for its nutritional benefits.

While in the frozen food section, it would be remiss to leave out man's best friend. Several manufacturers are producing frozen yoghurt treats for dogs. Meg Hanceford Meyer, one such producer, points out some of the reasoning behind this new trend. The premise is that on a hot day, eating a frozen treat is a great way to hydrate your dog, while adding nutrients to their diet. If it's good for our digestive health, then why wouldn't it be for your pet? Many markets are placing these pet-friendly frozen confections right next to those for people, so when you reach in the freezer, be sure you grab the right box for your species.

Counter Culture

No conversation about frozen yoghurt would be complete without delving into the counter culture – that is, the counter at your local yoghurt shop. The 1970s saw the advent of disco, 8-track players and frozen yoghurt. However, unlike the other two fads, frozen yoghurt (or 'froyo') is the only one that is still going strong. Froyo is especially popular in the u.s. and is now finding its place across the globe in local shops. While these stores are catching on worldwide, the u.s. accounts for 85 per cent of all soft-serve frozen yoghurt sales globally. At its height in the 1980s, frozen yoghurt enjoyed triple digit growth in the u.s., with sales reaching 25 million (that would be about 54 million when adjusting for inflation). Sales of frozen yoghurt remained consistent, with a big boost coming in the mid-2000s, when John Wudel developed live probiotic powders and brought the concept of soft-serve frozen yoghurt to a global market. Today it is a $2 billion industry in the u.s. alone.

A curious phenomenon contradicting taste preferences that almost doomed earlier frozen yoghurt treats is the popularity of tart frozen yoghurt. Red Mango, the brainchild of

Seoul-born Dan Kim, is a great example of this trend towards less-sweet frozen confections. Shelly Hwang and her partner Young Lee also seized on this craze and established Pinkberry. Much like the West Coast yoghurt wars between Yoplait and Dannon in the mid-1990s, Red Mango and Pinkberry more recently launched their own culture clash. Offering just a few flavours, with a variety of toppings, these companies were capitalizing on millennials' delight in something healthy and refreshing.

These chains began to pop up everywhere, and they gave way to yoghurt shops that feature self-serve dispensers. These shops began selling their products by weight, rather than as a single serving, and if you stroll into one, you will be astounded by the breadth of choices in both yoghurt flavours and toppings. 'Less is more' is not the mantra at these establishments, which account for about 69 per cent of the U.S. frozen yoghurt shops. Think of them as the 'all-you-can-eat midnight buffet' of yoghurt.

While self-serve yoghurt shops are ubiquitous in the U.S., most European countries still maintain storefronts in which you walk up to the counter and order from a menu of limited options. The IFYA (International Frozen Yogurt Association) is a treasure trove of frozen yoghurt information and the source for this global perspective. Let's start with an unusual offering, where Indonesia's Sour Sally was the first to bring froyo to that country. Sour Sally serves Black Sakura, frozen yoghurt with the addition of activated charcoal, said to be high in antioxidants. Sour Sally claims that it also flushes out toxins. The jury is out if that holds true. Greece's first frozen yoghurt shop, Froyo, which opened in Athens in 2010, sparked an initial boom there, with Chillbox earning the country's number-one spot today. Their frozen yoghurt has the qualities of their signature *straggisto*. Italy's entry into this space is

From healthy fruit to sugary sweets, yoghurt shops offer every mix-in imaginable to top your soft-serve frozen yoghurt.

Yogorino, which opened its first shop in 1993 and now boasts over one hundred locations in Italy and can be found in more than twenty countries across five continents. Italy's version is decidedly patterned after gelato, with a creaminess to rival. If you're in Mexico and have a hankering for frozen yoghurt, look for one of Nutrisa's 480 locations, and if you want to enjoy the frozen confection while watching your waistline, llaollao in Spain uses their proprietary skimmed milk called 'llao milk' in their one hundred stores. Australia is among the top ten countries selling frozen yoghurt, which all started when Wow Cow first established itself in 2007. Now the Yogurt Shop, Yogurtland and Yo-get-it join them in selling yoghurt to those Down Under.

According to Susan Linton, the force behind the International Frozen Yogurt Association (IFYA), frozen yoghurt stores are seeing growth across the board, with the Middle East becoming the most popular region per capita. The IFYA is the motivator behind America designating 6 February as the unofficial National Yoghurt Day, but it is trying to make it an international holiday with #IFYD International Frozen Yoghurt Day, to celebrate frozen yoghurt across the globe. It is hoping it catches on in the countries that enjoy frozen yoghurt worldwide. While the U.S. overwhelmingly leads the market, Europe is showing the most growth and predictions are that sales of frozen yoghurt are on an upward trajectory, growing about 3.4 per cent a year through 2024 with Canada, Greece, Brazil, Italy, Malaysia, Spain, the Philippines and Mexico trying to catch up with the U.S.

To stay on top, be on the lookout for the next big thing to hit the U.S. frozen yoghurt shop. For your consideration, at Reis & Irvy's, an American soft serve yoghurt shop, you can get some AI with your two scoops. Utilizing state-of-the-art technology, consumers are greeted by an interactive touch-screen that helps them order their chosen flavour and select toppings, and then in less than sixty seconds, a robot prepares the order. What's next? Perhaps someone to enjoy eating it for you!

6

Gut Reaction

In 2018 alone, more than 4,900 scientific publications explored yoghurt and your gut's microbiota. The research is cumbersome for the layperson and often one study contradicts or nullifies another. However, there are some correlations that cannot be denied when taken in the context of ongoing research and new daily developments. This chapter is here to help you interpret some of the major investigations and their conclusions. For those who crave statistics and scientific protocol, check out the reference section for where to find full articles that have provided the background for this chapter. A bit of caution: for every two studies showing yoghurt to be a magic bullet, there is another that says it is a dull sword. As with anything else you research, consider the source (many studies are self-promoting and funded by those with a vested interest), consider the size of the study and consider how it really relates to you. Then take this information before making any wholesale changes to your diet or lifestyle and ask a healthcare professional for their medically informed opinion.

While there exists research on every aspect of yoghurt consumption, contemporary studies focus on the most pressing: the impact yoghurt has on your immune system, CVD (cardiovascular disease), T2D (Type 2 diabetes) and obesity, and how it influences the brain–gut connection (the link between gastrointestinal health and mental outlook). Let's start with your immune system, as many in the medical community believe that health issues are immune related. The connection between yoghurt consumption and immunologic effects were carefully detailed by Simin Nikbin Meydani and Woel-Kyu Ha, who reviewed and analysed numerous studies aimed at identifying how and why yoghurt supports a healthy immune system. The researchers reported on many aspects of yoghurt's role in immunity from intestinal problems to cancer. They concluded that 'yogurt consumption and oral administration of LAB were shown to stimulate the host immune system.' They said that despite inconsistencies and some protocol issues, 'these studies provide a strong rationale for the hypothesis that increased yogurt consumption, particularly in immunocompromised populations such as the elderly, may enhance immunity.'[1]

By strengthening the gut, we also help mitigate inflammation, and scientists believe that when inflammation is controlled, the immune system can better control chronic disease. Brad Bolling, an assistant professor of food science at the University of Wisconsin-Madison, ran a study to focus on the role yoghurt might play in chronic inflammation and its relationship to the immune system. His results, after a nine-week study where half the subjects were fed yoghurt and the other half pudding, indicated that 'ongoing consumption of yogurt may be having a general anti-inflammatory effect'. He readily acknowledges more studies need to be conducted but was encouraged by the initial results.[2] This connection between yoghurt and immunity naturally leads us to the effect it might have on serious disease such as cancer. We know that yoghurt contains a very high level of CLA (conjugated linoleic acid), a healthy fatty acid present in dairy and meat from

A happy and healthy gut is no laughing matter.

ruminant animals. We know that CLA is enhanced through fermentation and further strengthened when the original source of the milk is grass fed. Its anticarcinogenic properties were examined in a National Academy of Science publication stating 'conjugated linoleic acid is the only fatty acid shown unequivocally to inhibit carcinogenesis in experimental animals.'[3] Therefore, it is not a huge leap to find that there is research in the linkage between yoghurt and fighting cancer. Mel Greaves, of London's Institute of Cancer Research, who was knighted in 2018 for his contribution to science, has spent a lifetime tackling the issue of childhood onset leukaemia. Greaves attributed an increase in the disease to a number of things, including 'a lack of exposure to microbes in early life that triggers an immune system malfunction which (in some cases) lead to acute lymphoblastic leukaemia (ALL) – the most common type of leukaemia'. Greaves is researching ways to strengthen a child's microbiome and 'block the chronic inflammation'. His ultimate goal is to 'create a yogurt-like drink that can stop children developing the disease in the first place'.[4]

There is tremendous interest in the correlation between yoghurt consumption and CVD. In a wide-sweeping study, reported in February 2018, it was concluded that 'higher long-term yogurt intake is associated with lower risk among hypertensive men and women.' The study followed a large cohort of more than 55,000 women and 18,000 men who had high blood pressure. It showed that among participants who consumed more than two servings a week of yoghurt in the context of a healthy diet, the risk for CVD was 17 per cent lower for women and 21 per cent lower for men, compared to those who consumed fewer than 1 serving a month.[5] Justin R. Buendia, one of the study's authors, went on to say, 'Our results provide important new evidence that yogurt may benefit heart health alone or as a consistent part of a diet rich in fiber-rich foods, vegetables, and whole grains.'[5]

In considering T2D (Type 2 Diabetes) and obesity, which are closely correlated, there is a plethora of ongoing research. In 2015 Amy Campbell in her article 'Two Thumbs up for Yogurt' reported on several studies related to these two conditions. The first, conducted at the University of Cambridge, looked at more than 25,000 people and found that those who ate yoghurt at least four and a half times per week were significantly at lower risk for T2D. And while yoghurt is not a cure for obesity, she referenced a comprehensive study conducted at the University of Navarra in Spain over a two-year period which looked at more than 8,000 Spanish men and women. The study showed a direct correlation between consuming seven or more servings a week of yoghurt and a decreased incidence of being overweight or obese. In another meta-analysis (one that looks at multiple studies and draws conclusions from all the data), the authors unequivocally gave yoghurt two-thumbs up, relative to T2D. Their study concludes: 'We found that higher intake of yogurt is associated with a reduced risk of T2D.'[6]

Frans Kok, Professor Emeritus and human nutrition expert at Wageningen University in the Netherlands, was quoted in a 2018 report published by Yogurt in Nutrition as to why yoghurt might have such a positive effect on weight: 'Proteins may influence appetite regulating hormones, calcium may affect fat absorption and live bacteria may alter gut microbiota – all of which may explain the beneficial effects that yogurt may have on body weight.'[7]

To make the best decisions, you need to use your brain, and yoghurt plays a role there too. With 70 per cent of your immune system and 90 per cent of all serotonin residing in your gut, to feel good, you need to keep your gut happy and healthy, and that's the premise behind much of the research in this area. There are more than 100 million brain cells in your gut, making the mind–gut connection very strong. Dr Jay Pasricha, director of the Johns Hopkins Center for Neuro-gastroenterology, explains the role of what is being termed the 'brain in your gut'. His research suggests that this 'second brain' is hidden in the walls of your digestive system and can affect everything from mood to anxiety, metabolism to cognition.[8] This premise has sparked lots of important research. A recent study from UCLA's School of Medicine found that those who ate probiotic yoghurt for a month actually showed measurable altered brain function. 'Our findings indicate that some of the contents of yoghurt may actually change the way our brain responds to the environment . . . "you are what you eat" and "gut feelings" take on new meaning,' said Dr Kirsten Tillisch, one of the lead researchers. Brain scans that measured brain activity showed definitive positive changes in those women who ate yoghurt as compared to those who did not.[9] Some posit that yoghurt can even change your perception of hunger. In a study published by Cambridge University Press, subjects were fed equal amounts of liquid yoghurt and chocolate and their satiety was rated. The study's authors concluded that 'satiety was perceived higher after liquid yogurt than chocolate bars', so next time you want to stave off hunger, reach for a yoghurt instead of the sweet stuff.[10]

To change gear here, a curious study that is fun to examine demonstrates some interesting results with regard to how yoghurt can make us (or our furry friends) feel. Research conducted in 2012 at MIT by immunobiologist Susan Erdman and geneticist Eric Alm studied forty male and forty female mice. One group ate 'junk', the other a typical mouse diet, with half the subjects in both groups being fed daily doses of yoghurt. The results were observationally noted by Erdman, who found 'yogurt-eating mice had very shiny coats . . . male mice had a sassy attitude . . . that sort of sexy swagger . . . In general, these were shiny, sexy mice.' The researchers went on to say 'mother mice that eat probiotics . . . have a higher success rate in raising their babies to weaning age with fewer events of maternal neglect.' They admit they are not sure why this is but propose that yoghurt-eating mice might have 'lower stress levels'. What was even more interesting was that it did not matter if the mice were on the typical or junk food diet; the changes were noticed across the board when yoghurt was eaten daily.[11]

Researchers in a presentation to the Sixth Global Summit on the Health Effects of Yogurt in 2019 reviewed numerous recent studies supportive that yoghurt is more than the sum of its parts. They stress that when considering yoghurt you have to consider its food matrix, the combined components in a particular food. They conclude that yoghurt's food matrix makes it 'a nutrient dense food that is an excellent source of high-quality protein and calcium as well as other minerals . . . and vitamins'. They go on to say that 'the health benefits of yogurt are derived from its nutrient composition, probiotic bacteria, and products of fermentation.'[12] Fermentation contributes to yoghurt being a low-density food, which means it provides fewer calories per gram. Yoghurt also utilizes its proteins efficiently because the fermentation process helps break down the proteins making them more easily digestible and the vitamins and minerals more bio-available. Eighty per cent of yoghurt proteins are caseins, which aid in the absorption of minerals. The balance is made up of whey, the yellowish liquid that is a by-product of the fermentation process. Whey has a high concentration of branched-chain amino acids (BCAA), which every athlete knows is great for muscle development and recovery, and is purported to be a great source of nourishment pre- and post-workout.

Yoghurt has been shown to do almost everything except help us brush our teeth – oh wait, New York City dentist Dr Steven Davidowitz did weigh in on yoghurt and dental health, citing the calcium in yoghurt as being very supportive of strong teeth, but the acidity as being the enemy of enamel. He suggests you should 'enjoy your yoghurt and then brush your teeth'. From hair masks to sunburn soother, acne-fighting properties to skincare regimens, yoghurt is a food that can literally do good from the outside in. Studies show it helps maintain bone strength, reduce the risk of allergies, treat intestinal issues and promote vaginal health. Perhaps most importantly, it allows lactose-intolerant people, who make up about 65 per cent of the world population and as many as 90 per cent among people of East Asian descent, to safely enjoy the benefits of milk.

7
Location, Location, Location

How you enjoy your yoghurt is intrinsically related to how your ancestors enjoyed theirs. Unlike many foods that gain traction because of an Instagram post by a social influencer, it is safe to assume most yoghurt influencers are someone's relative who has passed down their family traditions and recipes. In her article for the BBC travel blog, Madhvi Ramani quotes Elitsa Stoilova, a native from Bulgaria:

> If two grandmothers in different villages make yoghurt from the same products, the results will taste different. This is because yoghurt is an intimate product. It is linked to the land, the animals and the particular taste of the family and the knowledge of it is passed down from generation to generation.[1]

With this perspective in mind, it is no surprise that yoghurt remains integral to the diets of people living in the regions where yoghurt planted its roots. However, as people migrate, they take with them their culture (quite literally for some who use their family yoghurt culture brought over from another place). There is a global sharing of traditions and customs, tastes and aromas, preparations and inspirations that show-cases how the world seamlessly embraces this versatile food.

A multi-generational Bulgarian family pictured in 1912, when Bulgarian yoghurt was becoming a global phenomenon.

In a nod to the birthplace of *Lactobacillus bulgaricus*, let's start our global yoghurt journey in Bulgaria. There, our two famous strains synergistically create the gold standard of yoghurt, known in Bulgaria as *kiselo mlyako*. There is a uniquely proprietary acidic taste, creamy mouthfeel and distinguishing aroma that yoghurt aficionados can easily recognize as being Bulgarian. Strains from Bulgaria were being hawked, sold and shipped in the early and mid-1900s in freeze-dried or pill form. No better testament to reverence for Bulgarian yoghurt can be found than in a 1937 article in London's *The Observer*, in which was shared news of the closing of a small dairy shop in Salzburg. Apparently, people flocked to this Viennese store, including virtuoso conductor Arturo Toscanini, to delight in poetry and authentic Bulgarian yoghurt. A sample of verse from the shop's owner went like this:

Why are Bulgarians so old?
Why have they never got a cold?
Because they like to drink
Yoghurt in Winter and in Spring.

Bulgarian yoghurt holds a state patent, and Bulgarians license their eponymous strains to other countries, who, in order to call their yoghurt 'Bulgarian', must purchase their starter cultures from there. The best example of this relationship can be found between a small Bulgarian village in the Rhodope Mountains of Bulgaria and the Chinese. In 2009 China's

Chinese company Bright Dairy & Food launched Momchilovtsi ambient yoghurt drink in 2009 and it has been a top seller ever since.

Bright Dairy introduced an ambient yoghurt drink called Momchilovtsi, whose bacterial strains originated in the village of the same name. Produced in Shanghai and lovingly called Mosili'an in Chinese, it is the fastest-selling yoghurt product in China. Visit Momchilovtsi, the small village of its origin, and you will encounter signs in Chinese and self-taught Mandarin-speaking residents. Every year, there is a well-attended Chinese–Bulgarian festival, complete with a 'yoghurt queen'. The 1,200 inhabitants of the town, known as 'the village of longevity', entertain more than 1,000 Chinese visitors annually.

Another convergence of different global traditions influencing Chinese culture is the presence of yoghurt in the northern Chinese province of Xinjiang, where a large number of China's Uighurs reside. The Uighurs, of Muslim

Traditional Bulgarian festival in the Rhodope Mountains, where yoghurt is celebrated. Thousands of Chinese tourists visit every year.

Iconic Beijing yoghurt in its glass jars with traditional blue and white paper lid and straw.

Turkish descent, have lived there for more than 1,000 years. Their cuisine is more Middle Eastern than Han, with *nai lao* yoghurt being very popular.

As food writer Van notes on her blog FOOD *Is a Four-letter Word*,

> the original version (nai lao) of this was first learned by the imperial chefs in the 1800s, the recipe transformed into a more mild and sweeter version that caught on in Beijing in the 1950s when it became a hit among the health conscious and hip.[2]

The recipe spread throughout China, and today Beijing yoghurt is sold in every market and by vendors who line the busy streets. Enjoying Beijing yoghurt while strolling through the market is one of China's timeless traditions, in which thin straws or disposable spoons pierce the blue paper covers tied with string, and the yoghurt is enjoyed right there and then before the jars are returned to the vendor.

According to market analyst Tan Heng Hong, Chinese and Southeast Asian millennials are driving the yoghurt market as they look for exotic and beneficial pure yoghurt strains with probiotic benefits – if they come with a history and provenance, even better. Many Chinese consumers are wary of domestic dairy products, a result of a 2008 scandal related to the presence of melamine in the milk supply and infant formula. Melamine is an organic compound with strict limitations as a food additive. The incident caused the death of more than a dozen infants and mysteriously, four years after the scandal was revealed, the general manager of a dairy plant that was involved was rumoured to have been murdered in Xi'an city. In an effort to control the quality of their milk product, and in turn, the yoghurt that milk produces, China has begun to purchase farms and dairy cooperatives in France and Switzerland, as well as countries geographically closer to China such as New Zealand and Australia. As China has appropriated Western lifestyle choices, its citizens are focused greatly on the desire for protein and calcium-rich foods especially directed towards their children. This builds on the perception of yoghurt as not only being chock-full of health benefits, but something that strengthens immunity and provides the nutritional properties that this highly lactose-intolerant population cannot obtain otherwise.

Today's Chinese consumers are more urban, have more expendable income and are looking for portable sources of nutrition. The concept of on-the-go food really appeals to the Asian market, so throughout China and South Korea you will find women pedalling on bicycles to peddle yoghurt to a fast-moving population. South Korea's 'yoghurt ladies' wear signature apricot jackets and pink helmets. They drive motorized fridges called 'CoCos', short for 'Cold & Cool'. These refrigerators on wheels can hold an astounding 3,300 bottles of yoghurt. Yoghurt is still not seen as an ingredient or mainstream food in Asian cuisine, but rather a quick way to get a burst of nutrition. Statista, a market forecaster, reported that the China yoghurt sector generated u.s.$41.239 million in 2020 and is projected to grow 4.9 per cent annually through 2023. The China/Southeast Asian market is on pace to become the largest yoghurt-consuming market on the planet, with drinkable yoghurt helping to drive those numbers.

Not only are the Chinese discovering and rediscovering yoghurt, but other Asian markets are as well. Japan's love affair with yoghurt began in the 1930s, when a Kyoto-born scientist, Dr Minora Shirota, explored the connection between LAB and disease. After exhaustive research, he isolated *Lactobacillus casei Shirota* (LCS), a combination of more than three hundred types of LAB, which he used to ferment milk and called the product *Yakult*. The Japanese public embraced his product and his belief that a healthy intestine leads to a long life. Yakult is still widely enjoyed in Japan and by more than 30 million people around the globe daily, based on claims that it improves immunity and aids digestion. Japan came to the yoghurt market fully when dairy giant Meiji launched their first plain version in 1971. Much like the Chinese connection to Bulgaria, Meiji realized the Bulgarian connection would bolster sales and in 1973 obtained naming rights from Bulgaria, launching Meiji Bulgarian yoghurt. They continued innovating when in 1996 they acquired the rights to Japan's FOSHU (Food for Specified Health Use) label, which bolstered sales.[3]

More recently, Japan began enjoying a new range of flavoured yoghurts featuring such traditional deep-rooted ingredients as Matcha tea or persimmon. To further enhance the experience, the product is packaged in cups made to resemble ancient lacquerware. Yoghurt growth in Japan is predicted to continue, but with smaller growth spurts than seen in other parts of the Asian market.

On the Indian subcontinent, an area that includes India as well as parts of South and Central Asia, Pakistan, Bangladesh and the Himalayan states, yoghurt has been an integral part of local cuisine since ancient times. As a widely vegetarian culture, the people originating in this region consume yoghurt as a much-needed source of protein, calcium and fat. Additionally, yoghurt is a cooling food that tamps down the heat derived from the spices so popular in Indian cuisine. In India, yoghurt is called *dahi* (curd), where one strain of LAB is introduced to boiling rather than pasteurized milk. The goal of dahi is to encourage curd development, not to mitigate it, as many Western versions do. Making dahi is a daily activity in which the curd from the day before is added to a new batch, resulting in a thick and tangy yoghurt.

Curd is the foundation for many of India's iconic dishes. It helps bring together rice and *dal* (a soupy lentil/pea dish), making it easier to pick up and eat with your right hand – Indian style. *Aloo palda*, a potato curry with curd, relies on yoghurt to help achieve the texture needed to bind this classic Pahari dish. In *mor rasam*, a sour curd is used to create the signature buttermilk-like taste, while *dahi papdi chaat* highlights a blend of yoghurt with a variety of chutneys, such as mint and coriander or tamarind, that top this popular pick-up food. Yoghurt finds its way into soft *dosas* (lentil/rice dumplings) and *biryani*, a speciality of Kashmir, which is a slow-cooked stew traditionally prepared on a *dum* (a sealed, heavy-bottomed vessel). There's even an Indian version of grilled cheese that combines yoghurt with onions, spices and herbs to create dahi toast, a popular breakfast offering.

Dahi is so integral to Hindu culture that on the day following Janmashtami, in observance of Krishna's birth, dahi Handi (meaning curd in an earthen pot) is celebrated with youths forming a pyramid to reach a pot filled with yoghurt and other goodies.

Chicken Biryani: definitely not fast food, but it is fabulous food.

Traditional mango lassi with a low-tech Indian blending pot.

Possibly the best-known of all Indian dishes featuring yoghurt is *raita*, a cooling mix of yoghurt and a variety of mix-ins, from vegetables to fruits, herbs to spices. It is both a condiment and a side dish and is 'oh so simple' to make. India's national drink, the *lassi*, is a yoghurt-based smoothie, with origins dating back to around 1000 BCE from the Punjab region. It can be enjoyed in a salty version with ground cumin or red chilli, or satisfyingly sweet with the addition of mango or rose water.

Speaking of sweets, do not overlook the sublime simplicity of Maharashtra's classic dessert *shrikhand*, which needs only three ingredients: *chakka* (strained yoghurt), powdered sugar and the crunch of dry fruit. It is a vessel of flavour, as it can be infused with saffron strands, perked up with cardamom or topped with pistachios.

In Indonesia, people enjoy *dadiah*, the Indonesian take on yoghurt made from unheated buffalo milk, which ferments in a bamboo shoot. And in Nepal, people enjoy their yoghurt as part of cultural and religious celebrations. The Nepalese believe that yoghurt, called *juju dhai*, can impart good luck; therefore, clay pots filled with their version are often placed at an entrance way to greet celebrants. You don't need to be

Herbaceous and delicious raita is a perfect dip or condiment.

Shrikhand is a delicious dessert from Maharashtrian and Gujarati cuisine of India.

Kefir can be enjoyed in many ways, including as a delicious drink with fresh herbs.

living in these countries to enjoy any of these iconic yoghurt dishes, as the cooking style that defines this cuisine has fused with other styles and is enjoyed throughout the Middle East, Southeast Asia, Europe, North America, Africa and the Caribbean.

In the Caucasus Mountains, yoghurt is enjoyed in a variety of ways, with the most popular being a drink called *kefir*. This fermented beverage is not quite yoghurt's sibling, more like a close cousin. It can be made from the milk of cows, sheep or goats and differs from yoghurt in that kefir grains (which is a misnomer, because they're not really grains at all) are added to the process and cause a slightly bubbly, carbonated result. Termed 'the champagne of cultured dairy products', kefir is gaining ground in the u.s. and the uk, where it is seen as a healthy alternative to soda. Like yoghurt, it is nutrient-dense, but its wide variety of bacteria ferments at room temperature, it has a very slight alcohol content and contains active yeast, which imparts its own benefits and clearly distinguishes it from yoghurt. Almost as far away from the Caucasus

Kefir grains.

as you can get is Chile, where people are discovering kefir, or, as they call it, 'birds' yoghurt'. Immigrants from Russia introduced the drink to this part of the world. Kefir can easily be brewed at home with grains purchased online, at health food stores or in a variety of food shops.

The people of Central Asia and Mongolia have also enjoyed drinking their yoghurt for millennia in the form of *koumiss* (*kumys*, *kumis*, *kumiss*). The word for this product is Turkish in origin; it is a fermented milk with an alcohol content of about 3 per cent, which might make you tipsy, but is found in the dairy aisle, not the beer section. It was originally made from mare's milk and had a lovely sweet taste. The additional sucrose in the milk accounted for the alcohol content

Akim Polikarpovich Kurochkin, photograph of Yakut woman (Turkic ethnic group residing in Sakha Republic, Russian Federation) ladling *koumiss* (*kymys*) during the Yhyakh festival, Namsky district, April 1913.

Ayran is traditionally served in a copper mug and is a refreshing complement to Turkish food.

being higher than fermented products made from the milk of other animals. Today koumiss is commercially prepared with cow's milk, as mare's milk can be hard to come by. The product is gently sweetened to replicate the original flavour and effervescent quality. Explorer William of Rubrick, who in 1250 journeyed across the steppes of Mongolia, kept an extensive diary of his travels, which were carefully translated in 1900. Of this intoxicating drink, he said, 'Koumiss makes the inner man most joyful.'

Yoghurt continues to be integral to the cuisine of Turkey, the region where it first originated. It is a favourite ingredient, condiment and side dish and the foundation for Turkey's most famous beverage, *ayran*. Thought to have been discovered by the Göktürks (a nomadic group of Turkic peoples), ayran is essentially watered-down yoghurt that produces lactic acid, but no alcohol. It was especially useful in the hot summer months as the nomads endured the desert heat. Ayran would refresh and replenish, as salt is traditionally added to the drink. Turks and many others in the region continue to enjoy aryan today, so much so that if you wander into a local McDonald's, it will most likely be on the menu. The Turks also enjoy a dish very similar to India's raita, but with their own twist. Yoghurt is diluted and combined with salt, crushed garlic, cucumber, mint and dill, and often sumac, lime juice and olive oil. The result is *cacik,* a dip-like preparation that is refreshing and cooling. This is the perfect condiment for so many of the Turkish specialities like kebabs and koftas, the Turkish interpretation of the meatball.

But yoghurt goes much deeper into the cuisine of Turkey and finds its way into *kahvalti*, a Turkish breakfast feast in which sweets are shunned and offerings such as *cilbir*, a dish of yoghurt mixed with fresh crushed garlic and salt, is generously poured over poached eggs. You cannot discuss Turkish food without mentioning *manti*, their version of ravioli. These tiny dumplings are stuffed with spicy ground lamb, minced chicken or ground beef and swim in a yoghurt sauce often spiked with garlic, chilli pepper, mint and rosemary. The Turks have their own strained yoghurt called *suzme*, which is thick and unctuous and is found on most meze platters. Suzme functions as a perfect marinade for meat, as it coats the meat, and its acidic properties serve not only as a flavour enhancer, but as a tenderizing agent. It can be gently heated and pairs especially well with goat or lamb stew, where it adds a sour note, and when combined with flour, serves as a slurry or thickener. Vegetarian favourites such *ekşili pilav*, a traditional

Dried *tarhana* (top), and the velvety soup it can create.

dish of bulgur rice, tomato and herbs, benefit from yoghurt's assertive taste, and it is a natural with slow-simmered or fried aubergine. A signature dish of Turkey is *tarhana*, the term for yoghurt that is combined with grains and often vegetables, which are fermented and dried into coarse crumbs. Tarhana is also the name of the iconic soup made from rehydrating that is an Anatolian staple.

When not fulfilling its savoury destiny, yoghurt is a key ingredient in some of Turkey's most beloved desserts. It can be simply swirled with honey and poppy seeds or baked into a *revani*, a type of yoghurt cake that has been around since the Ottoman Empire.

A Persian version of watered-down yoghurt, similar to ayran, is called *doogh*, often using a sparkling water to create a fizzy experience. Doogh was also most likely discovered and consumed by the Göktürks, hence its name originates from the Turkish word for 'milking'. The addition of mint or cucumber helps to mask the bitter taste and add a spirited

Bottles of *doogh* on Haraz Road, Mazandaran, Iran.

note. This yoghurt soda is produced traditionally at home, but bottled Abali Yogurt Soda is readily available online. A recent source of pride is doogh being included in the Codex Alimentarius, making it an internationally registered and recognized drink. So ingrained is sour milk in Persian culture that in modern-day Iran, the expression 'mind your own business' translates to 'Go beat your own yoghurt.' Persians introduce yoghurt in almost every way imaginable, such as in *ashe-mâst*, a warm yoghurt soup with fresh herbs, spinach and lentils.

Scandinavians have a long history of enjoying yoghurt. Their cold, sometimes harsh climate has necessitated creative ways to prolong the shelf life of dairy. They enjoy a slightly thick, yoghurt-like drink called *filmjölk*, colloquially known as *fil*, which has been around since the Viking era, in the first century. Filmjölk is fermented differently from yoghurt, so they differ in taste, but it is chock-full of probiotic bacteria and is regarded by some as one of the secrets of a healthy Swedish diet. Scandinavians also grab a spoon and eat *villi*, a Nordic fermented yoghurt created with mesophilic bacteria that incubates at a lower temperature. This process creates a thin layer of mould on top and accounts for *villi*'s unique taste, aroma and appearance. It produces exopolysaccharides (EPS), stringy, cord-like yoghurt, which Edith Salminen of the Nordic Food Lab calls 'ropy milks of Scandinavia', or 'slime!'.[4] Switching from spoon to straw, Scandinavians relish *piimä*, their yoghurt version of buttermilk, with its cheese-like taste. And, of course, there's *skyr*, Scandinavia's 'oh-so-thick', traditional plain yoghurt. Nordic people consume an average of 100 g (3½ oz) of yoghurt a day, and while there are many versions of these 'ropy milks', they each have their own flavour and acidity, creating unique mouthfeel and taste. While you might not find these in your local market – unless, of course, you live in a Scandinavian country – cultures to create Nordic yoghurt at home are readily available online.

The African continent has several yoghurt versions that are a mainstay of nutrition in a largely lactose-intolerant society. In Kenya, *mursik* is a fermented yoghurt drink that incubates in a hollowed-out calabash gourd. Prior to the addition of cow's or goat's milk, the gourd is treated with ash from an indigenous tree known for its antiseptic properties. After several days of fermenting, the whey is drained, and the gourd is vigorously shaken, with more ash added as a flavour enhancer. The result is a slightly greyish-blue drink, with a silky texture and an acidic flavour. *Amasi* is a South African version, which the Zulu people consider a source of strength and endurance, and it has an interesting connection to Nelson Mandela. Amasi is the thick portion that remains after the whey is drained from the fermented milk and is often poured over grains or porridge. It is said that while hiding out in a white neighbourhood, Mandela could not forego his amasi. He left a glass of milk to ferment on a windowsill, which tipped off locals that a person of African heritage was living there, something that certainly seemed uncommon during apartheid. When Mandela overheard some workers questioning the presence of the fermenting liquid in a white neighbourhood, he made a fast exit to avoid being discovered.

Greece has literally made a name for itself in the world of yoghurt, and as we know, it is often imitated. For the real thing, you need to try *straggisto*, authentic strained Greek yoghurt, in the place of its birth. The luscious product finds its way into many Greek recipes, the best-known being *tzatziki,* a culinary cousin of *raita*. The simple preparation combines grated cucumbers that are drained of their liquid, mixed with yoghurt, crushed mint, olive oil, salt and a squeeze of lemon juice. When the flavours meld, it is a terrific accompaniment

In Greece, tzatziki is an appetizer (meze), or used as a sauce.

to many hearty Greek specialities. While Greek yoghurt was not trademarked by Greece, the EU routinely sanctions countries that label their yoghurt as 'Greek', claiming that it deliberately misleads the consumer. As if additional proof of yoghurt's prominence in Greece were needed, it was reported that in 1948, on his deathbed, Greek Premier Themistocles Soufoulis requested his final meal and promptly downed two glasses of beer, a bowl of soup and his beloved yoghurt.

Yoghurt goes by many names in the Arab and Middle Eastern world, including *zabady*, *laban zabady*, *roba* and *laban rayeb*. In this part of the world, there is a rich history of producing yoghurt, traditionally made by boiling water buffalo milk and culturing it with starter from a previous batch. Middle Eastern yoghurt features a skin that forms on the surface and a delectable fatty rich creamy layer that rises to the top. The delicacy is associated with the all-day fasting during Ramadan, as it is thought to prevent thirst. Perhaps the best-known yoghurt product in the Middle East is *labneh*, a staple of that cuisine, with a firm cream cheese texture often compared to quark, a cheese-like yoghurt popular in German and Slavic cultures. Labneh is thoroughly strained, releasing all the whey with the help of a bit of salt. Labneh can almost always be found on a meze plate as a dip, a creamy spread on pita or as a best friend for zaatar, a spicy blend of aromatics. In Israel, labneh is a key ingredient in salads, stirred with figs and honey or tossed with grains. Michael

Yoghurt and freshly prepared zhoug, a spicy green sauce popular in Middle Eastern cooking, mix together in a delicious blend.

Félix Bonfils, photograph of Arab women in Jerusalem carrying containers filled with labne(h), *c.* 1890.

Solomonov, an award-winning chef and unofficial ambassador of Israeli cuisine, cites labneh among a handful of Israeli foundational ingredients that also includes tahini and lemon.

In a nod to tzatziki, Middle Eastern cooks have their version called *mâst-o-khâir*, made with cucumber, spring onions and herbs, and it is used as a palate cleanser. It has light, refreshing notes and makes a great side to grilled meats. Yoghurt is a principle ingredient in *shakriya*, an Arabic dish with cubes of lamb, beef or bison, to which it adds tartness and creaminess to the preparation. It tempers the heat when spooned over chicken curry or becomes a focal point in a traditional Levantine breakfast of spicy chickpeas and crispy pita. Salty yoghurt pairs perfectly with a dal made from onions, split peas, coriander, turmeric, cardamom and red pepper flakes and wakes up pretty much any Middle Eastern grain. Perhaps one of the most interesting uses of yoghurt is in Jordan's national dish, *mansaf*. In this dish, lamb is cooked in a tangy sauce of *jameed* (fermented dried yoghurt) and lavishly plated atop thin flatbread. As is the tradition of the region, celebrations often include mansaf, which is served at a communal table, as people scoop up rice and the mansaf with three fingers, with their left hands tucked behind their backs. No celebration is necessary to enjoy Middle Eastern desserts where

Mansaf, Jordan's national food, features yoghurt prominently.

With its inviting yellow colour, tart hint of lemon and savoury yoghurt on top and in the cake, this Middle Eastern semolina cake hits all the right notes.

yoghurt is the star, however. Try baking *hareesa* (not to be confused with the North African chilli paste harissa), a semolina cake with yoghurt, the crunch of almonds, sweetness of rosewater and a hint of lemon.

By the Numbers

Understanding that yoghurt is enjoyed in every corner of the world, not everyone everywhere enjoys yoghurt to the same extent. Here's a quick-speed round of statistics, based on a DSM (a global manufacturer of food enzymes and ingredients) 2016 survey of 6,000 men and women in six major markets. Seventy-three per cent of French people enjoy yoghurt on its own for dessert, while 77 per cent of Turkish eaters pair it with a warm meal. In Poland, 51 per cent prefer flavoured yoghurt and eat it as a snack. In China, most drink their yoghurt, in a market that grew by over 110 per cent in the middle of this decade, with only 11 per cent digging in with a spoon.

Chinese consumers were also the largest group who buy yoghurt for its probiotic features, roughly 83 per cent as compared to 50 per cent or less worldwide. This accounts for the whopping 108 per cent increase in yoghurt consumption among the Chinese in 2013–17. As for Brazil, people here enjoy yoghurt with cereal 55 per cent of the time, with flavoured yoghurt being the choice of 45 per cent of consumers. In the u.s yoghurt is still not seen as a daily dose of goodness, with only 6 per cent saying they enjoy yoghurt every day, 36 per cent of whom choose Greek yoghurt over other styles. Germans, Italians and Polish people mostly consume their yoghurt at breakfast, but it is in the u.s. where 93 per cent report that breakfast is the meal in which they eat theirs. The British still enjoy their yoghurt, but less than they used to.

A 2018 report in *The Telegraph* noted that Brits are consuming significantly less yoghurt, down nearly 11 million servings at dinner and a whopping 73 million at lunch. The report also noted that in 2016, children ate yoghurt on 82 million fewer occasions. But not so in France, where they wouldn't think of missing their daily serving. For the French, yoghurt is a religion. Jacqueline Dubois Pasquier, journalist for My French Life (www.myfrenchlife.org) shared with me via email the role yoghurt plays in what she terms 'the French eating habits landscape': 'yoghurt has been as important as cheese.' In many French and European households, an astounding 30 kg (65–70 lb) of yoghurt is consumed per person (compared with 6.5 kg (14 lb) in America, and 10 kg (2 lb) in Canada). Jacqueline notes that millennials in France are driving the options for plant-based yoghurt but she believes that the French are not ready yet to sacrifice 'taste' to health. As new varieties of yoghurt are introduced, it will be interesting to see if these numbers and trends continue.

8

Homemade Yoghurt: From Formulation to Infatuation

Little Miss Muffet, sat on her tuffet eating her curds
and whey, along came a spider who sat down beside her
and frightened Miss Muffet away.
'Mother Goose'

It is entirely possible that the Little Miss Muffet namesake of
the 1600s French nursery rhyme might have abandoned her
curds and whey because she knew how to make more at
home. While there are countless options in your dairy aisle to
choose from, all yoghurt devotees must try, at least once, to
make their own homemade yoghurt. As Ralph Waldo Emerson wrote, 'Adopt the pace of nature; her secret is patience.'[1]
That perfectly describes the Zen experience of brewing your
own batch, creating yoghurt with the taste and texture you
want, and nothing you don't. No added sugar, salt, thickeners
or modifiers. Just pure, slightly tart, mildly tangy, deliciously
thick yoghurt. As Claudia Roden explains in her beautiful
cookbook *The New Book of Middle Eastern Food*, 'with a little
experience one learns the rhythm of preparation and the
exact warmth required to turn milk into yogurt. The actual
preparation is extremely easy, but the right conditions are

necessary for success. If these are fulfilled, the "magic" cannot fail.'[2] Here's how to approach making your own magic with a bit of rhyme: formulate, percolate, inoculate, incubate, refrigerate, perpetuate!

Formulate

For cow's milk yoghurt, here's what you need to get started. The most important ingredients are good fresh milk and fresh starter culture. Whole organic milk will create thick, creamy yoghurt, but you can use skimmed or low-fat milk if you prefer. If you choose to use anything less than whole milk, you might want to add non-fat dry milk to help create more structure. You can also follow the trend and add cream to your milk base for a luxuriously rich finish. Do not use ultra-pasteurized or ultra-filtered milk, as they have been heat treated at too high a temperature, killing off much of the milk's necessary enzymes. Raw milk can also be used, but its unheated bacteria could be harmful, as well as compete with your starter. Proponents of raw milk would disagree, so you can decide what's best for you. Alternatives to cow's milk and plant-based options can be used as well but require a bit more effort to achieve the right texture and consistency. Essentially, any milk, when the right bacteria is introduced, will ferment. For the bacteria, you can start your first batch by using plain, shop-bought yoghurt that contains live and active cultures. You can also purchase cultures in a variety of combinations at most health food shops or online from a reputable source. For resources on where to learn more about these options, check the Websites and Associations section at the end of this book.

Percolate

You can use any pot to brew your yoghurt, but stainless steel will help mitigate build-up when the milk is heated. Try rubbing a few ice cubes in your pot before adding the milk – the layer of cold will prevent build-up as well. For the best results, you need to heat your milk slowly and be sure it reaches 80°C (180°F). This warming process helps denature (break down) the milk proteins, setting them up to coagulate

Patience, a stainless-steel pot, a non-reactive spoon and a thermometer are what you need when heating your yoghurt.

nicely; additionally, it kills any competing bacteria in your milk, allowing your starter to work its magic.

For a thicker yoghurt, hold the milk at 80°C (180°F) for at least ten and up to thirty minutes. This should be more than adequate to give you a thick result. However, you can add non-fat dry milk to create even more structure – try 115 g (½ cup) per 2 litres (½ gallon) of milk, and add more or less to achieve your desired final consistency. Another method to add viscosity and a rich finish would be to replace some of the milk with cream. As for tools, an instant-read thermometer is really helpful, but you can use visual cues to determine when the milk is heated to the right temp. A film will begin to form, and tiny bubbles emerge – that's the point right before boiling and indicates your milk is heated properly. Stir

Enjoy this film that collects on the surface of the heated milk, as many do as a side benefit of making home-made yoghurt.

your milk occasionally as it heats, removing the film that forms and discarding it. Alternatively, you can put it aside, as many in the UK do, and spread it on a scone – it acts much like clotted cream. In India, that film is called *malai* and can be added to tea or milk for that extra-special something. If you heat the milk too high, not to worry – simply lower the heat, let it come back down to 80°C (180°F), and go from there. Once you've completed this step, it's time to move on to cooling and then inoculating the yoghurt.

Inoculate

The milk is now properly heated, the proteins have been broken down, and it is primed for your starter. Now comes the most crucial step: inoculating the yoghurt. Remove your pot of milk from the heat and allow it to cool down to 45°C (115°F). If you add your starter at too high a temperature, the heat will kill it; if it's added when the milk is too cold, it won't activate. There are several ways to speed up this cooling process. You can place the pot in an ice bath or sink filled with cold water, or wrap the pot in a frozen gel pack that you might have on hand for a sore knee or shoulder. Be sure to take the pot out of the ice bath or unwrap it when it reaches 50°C (120°F), as the residual cooling effect could cause the temperature to drop below your desired 45°C (115°F). If you don't mind waiting, simply take the pot off the hob, go and read a book or clean out a cupboard, and come back in about 45 minutes; the milk should be ready to inoculate. Check your milk periodically, either with your thermometer or by dipping a clean finger into the pot to test the temperature. If you can comfortably hold your finger there for ten seconds, it has cooled enough. Whichever method you choose, be sure to set

Set a timer, grab a thermometer and allow your milk to cool to just the right temperature.

a timer and become familiar with how long it takes for your milk to cool down. Once you do, it will just be rote for the next time.

If using a shop-bought yoghurt as a starter, while you wait for the milk to cool down, remove the yoghurt from the fridge and place 2 tbsp (for 2 l/½ gallon of milk) in a small bowl and set aside. If you are using freeze-dried starter, please follow the manufacturer's directions, as some need to be activated before using. When making yoghurt, less is more. Do not make more than 2 l (½ gallon) at a time. Too large a quantity of milk might make it harder to maintain the correct temperature while heating and incubating. Do not add more starter thinking it will make your yoghurt better. It will actually crowd the bacteria and prevent them from performing their fermenting destiny. Once the milk has cooled, take a ladleful of the milk and add it to the yoghurt you set aside. Stir and pour this back into your pot. By tempering the yoghurt, you are helping to gently introduce it to the warmed milk.

Incubate

Incubating your yoghurt is a real exercise in patience. Your yoghurt needs to rest in a warm, undisturbed place for at least five and up to twelve hours at a temperature that ranges from 35°C to 45°C (95°F to 115°F). There are so many methods to incubate yoghurt, and you should explore more than one to see which suits you the best. The oven light method is pretty sure-fire, as the ambient heat from the light maintains just the right temperature for fermentation. Take your pot or whatever container you choose to incubate in (just be sure it is dishwasher clean), pour the inoculated milk into it, cover the pot or container, wrap it in a towel, place it in the oven with the light on, and leave it for the prescribed time. Be sure to put a sign on your oven so that no one mistakenly turns it on and ruins your batch.

Alternatives to this method include wrapping the container in a heating pad at the low setting, or filling a polystyrene cooler with bottles of hot water to keep the yoghurt company and maintain the correct temperature. You can even ferment yoghurt in a thermos that can retain heat for the necessary time, or place the container on a coffee warmer or hot plate at the lowest setting. Prior to incubating, be sure to test the temperature of the method you plan to use, to be certain it is neither too hot nor too cold. If using mesophilic starter that does not require heat activation, you can ferment your yoghurt on your counter top, maintaining a temperature between 20°C and 45°C (between 70°F and 115°F) for about twelve hours. Of course, Instant Pots and yoghurt makers have made simple work of preparing yoghurt, and if you own one, go ahead and use that foolproof method, following the manufacturer's directions.

For your first batch, test it after five–six hours and jiggle the pot. If it pulls away from the sides and has a gel-like texture, some liquid (whey) on top or where the curd is separated, and smells like yoghurt, it's done. However, for a thicker or tarter finish, you can let it sit for even longer. Relying on a billion microorganisms isn't always replicable, so your yoghurt might be a touch tarter, or a bit runnier, depending on the

This home-made yoghurt maker from an industrious yoghurt fan demonstrates how ambient light is enough to ferment yoghurt.

When a spoon can stand to attention in your yoghurt, you know it is going to be thick and creamy.

potency of the bacteria, the heat differentiation in your incubation and the amount of time you held the milk. You'll always have yoghurt, but it's actually a fun surprise to taste the slight variations from time to time. At the end of the day, even a less-than-perfect batch of homemade yoghurt beats shop-bought yoghurt. Once you get your timing and routine down, it will be smooth sailing. Additionally, different starters have different end results, so experiment with Bulgarian on Finnish, traditional or Greek starters to find which tickles your taste buds.

Refrigerate

But wait, do not taste your yoghurt yet; it will definitely disappoint. Let the yoghurt sit out in your container for about an hour. This helps it acclimatize to your fridge when you place it in there to fully chill and set. Once cool and ready to eat, should your yoghurt have any lumps, simply stir in one or two ice cubes and whisk – the lumps should disappear. This is a common problem and the result of either heating the milk too fast or incubating it too long or at too warm a temperature. If the yoghurt doesn't set up properly, try holding the milk at 80°C (180°F) a little longer or heating the milk more slowly next time. It might also be because your starter was too weak, or the incubation process was stopped too soon. Again, this is definitely an 'if at first you don't succeed, try, try again' endeavour. Generally, your yoghurt can last up to two weeks in the fridge, but it does lose potency the longer it sits. You know it has spoilt when it has an 'icky' smell, funky appearance or tastes off. So making less yoghurt more often is the rule of thumb. You can also freeze it, and it should keep nicely for about two months.

You can easily create Greek yoghurt from your batch. You will need cheesecloth, muslin or large coffee filters, a strainer and a bowl to collect the whey. Simply line the strainer with your filter of choice and place it over a bowl. If straining for under three hours, you can leave it on your counter. Drain one hour to remove 20 per cent of the whey, three–four hours to remove 50 per cent, or overnight or eight hours to remove almost all the whey. If you add a touch of salt and strain your yoghurt for 24 hours in the fridge, you can create labneh, a very thick, spreadable yoghurt-cheese.

Remember: no way should you discard the whey you collect. Technically, whey is milk with all the fats and solids

Draining the whey requires nothing more than a filter, a strainer, a bowl and time.

pulled out, so it does contain lactose milk sugar. Use it to make protein-packed smoothies or lacto-fermented veggies, or to marinate meat and poultry. You can basically substitute whey for water or other liquids in most recipes, adding not only lots of nutrients, but a slightly tangy taste. It makes a terrific base for homemade stock: just add bones and veggies and brew for several hours. But wait, there's way more. Home gardeners can use whey to invigorate their gardens, as it is full of nitrogen, and for plants that require additional acidity, it's the way to go. You can even spray it on plants to ward off mildew – a way to outsmart Mother Nature. Many yoghurt manufacturers are selling their whey to dairy farmers to feed the cows that produce the milk that creates the yoghurt. How's that for the way to pay it forward? And for those who like to take lingering baths, some say it will even soften your skin. Cleopatra was said to have bathed in whey, so while it sounds 'way out', it might actually be luxuriating.

Perpetuate

Be sure to scoop off 60 ml (¼ cup) of your yoghurt as your next starter. Do this before you add any fruit or sweetener, as you don't want to diminish its potential to restart a new batch. To use as a starter, keep it in a sealed container in your fridge for up to seven days or in your freezer for up to two months. Thaw your yoghurt before using it to start a new batch, and never use refrigerated yoghurt older than seven days as a starter. Get in the habit of labelling the container with a date, so you know when it has lost its potential to restart your next batch. Traditional starter, resulting from store-bought yoghurt, can re-culture through about six–seven cycles before it will lose its oomph. Simply buy a new container or packet and begin anew. Heirloom culture, which contains a higher concentration and variety of bacteria, can be used as starter culture indefinitely. Think of regular starter as a thread that can be tugged just so many times before tearing, while heirloom culture is like a spiderweb of threads that have support and structure and hold together. If you follow these steps and the dos and don'ts below, you will be rewarded with delectable results and instant infatuation.

Do
1. Use the freshest ingredients.
2. Be patient.
3. Try different milk sources.
4. Do experiment with a variety of starter cultures.
5. Make homemade yoghurt a regular practice.

Don't
1. Rush a step.
2. Tamper with your yoghurt until it's time.

3. Add too much of anything to your finished yoghurt.
4. Forget to save some for future use.
5. Get discouraged.

When searching online for variations, methods to ferment milk alternatives or troubleshooting, be selective. With everyone having access to a keyboard, there is a lot of misinformation floating around. Please feel free to visit my website, www. junehersh.com, for tips. I am here to help from percolation to perpetuation and right on into infatuation!

Final Thoughts

When I began this book, I will confess, I was an occasional yoghurt eater. Like the typical American, it was not part of my daily dietary routine, but rather a fast breakfast for those days when time just wouldn't allow making an omelette or whipping up a batch of pancakes. But that was then, and this is now. I can truly say after researching this timeless food and preparing countless batches, I am a yoghurt devotee. I hesitate to cite another food with the same rich history and impact on evolution as yoghurt. Few foods have such a broad cultural identity, profile of sustainability, vast array of options or versatility. Once you welcome these millions of microorganisms into your life and your gut you will find dozens of ways to enjoy it and scientific evidence that it is actually making you healthier and happier. Yoghurt is not a cure-all medicinal supplement or answer to every malady we face. But it is an easy way to strengthen your microbiome naturally and deliciously. It is the perfect protein vehicle for those who are sensitive to lactose, it is a wonderful first food for children, it is an easy substitute for less healthy food choices, whether it be in cooking or baking. Yoghurt is a food that carnivores and vegans can agree on, and one that you can easily prepare at home and enjoy endlessly. It will be interesting to see where the yoghurt industry goes and what your dairy aisle

As fresh as a country spring day, this yoghurt semifreddo is a crowd-pleaser.

will look like into this decade. Will plant-based and vegan options outweigh traditional dairy? Will exotic flavours overtake the current leader – strawberry – as the flavour du jour? Will drinkable versions outrank spoonable and the war on sugar truly make inroads in cutting back or eliminating altogether those less than healthy options for kids and adults? Michael Pollan, in his defining work *In Defense of Food* (2008), implores us, 'Don't eat anything your great grandmother wouldn't recognize as food.'[1] Might that very good advice inform us to shun 'fake' food and go back to our ancestral roots and brew our own batches of fermented goodness? Processed food with its carbon footprint overload could become a thing of the past and sustainable, functional foods such as yoghurt could see an even more meteoric rise globally. Fuelled by the Southeast Asian market, influenced by the desire for probiotic rich sources of nearly lactose-free energy, and emboldened by further research to support its healthy qualities, yoghurt just might steal the spotlight from kombucha, cauliflower rice and oat milk lattes. Here's to the next millennium of enjoying yoghurt, taking it from Neolithic times to modern times and beyond: enjoy it in good health!

Recipes

Basic Cow's Milk Yoghurt

Preparation time: Under 30 minutes
Inactive Time: 5–12 hours depending on length of incubation
Yields: 2 l (½ gallon, 65 oz)

2 l whole milk (organic preferred)
2 tbsp store-bought or homemade plain yoghurt containing
live and active cultures

Heat the milk in a large, uncovered pot over medium heat, until an instant-read thermometer registers 80°C (180°F). Stir occasionally to prevent a film from forming. Hold the milk at 80°C (180°F) for at least 10 and up to 30 minutes. Remove the pot from the hob and allow it to cool to 45°C (115°F). Remove your starter yoghurt from the fridge and measure 2 tbsp into a small bowl; set aside. When the yoghurt is at 45°C (115°F), stir one ladle of the cooled milk into the bowl with the starter yoghurt; whisk gently, and add to the large pot. Incubate using one of the described methods. Refrigerate and enjoy.

Vintage Recipes

These classic and simple recipes show how easy it was then and still is now to include yoghurt in quick preparations. Because they are of a different era, most don't conform to the way current recipes are presented. They're just like the recipe your great-grandmother has handed down to you, scribbled on a worn and torn piece of paper with inexact measurements and directions. But, they are timeless, so enjoy.

Sour Milk Soup
from Mildred Grosberg, *The Jewish Cookbook* (New York, 1947)

Let 1 quart of sour milk stand until it jellies, but does not separate. Put it in a saucepan and simmer 1 minute. Melt 1 tbsp butter in another saucepan; add 2 generous tbsp of flour and stir until they bubble.

Add the milk and stir until smooth. Strain through a fine sieve. Sprinkle a spoonful of grated maple sugar over the top of each serving

Yoghurt Salad Dressing
When yoghurt began to gain popularity worldwide, articles with 'exotic' recipes began cropping up. The *Honolulu Advertiser* published this one on 4 January 1951, with its grammatically awkward title *Yoghurt Salad Dressing Good*. The introduction to the recipe said your guests will question 'That strange and wonderful new flavour in this salad dressing – what is it?' They go on to say the dressing will 'glorify the simplest salad ingredients'.

Ingredients
120 ml (½ cup) mayonnaise or salad dressing
120 ml (½ cup) Yami Yogurt (just as it comes in the jar) or your favourite brand
60 ml (¼ cup) ketchup
120 ml (½ cup) Indian relish

Mix ingredients together quickly and thoroughly. Season with salt and all-purpose seasoning, Simply serve on hearts of lettuce – and listen to the family rave!

Orange Yoghurt Pops

Not to be outdone, in June 1961 the *Freeport Journal*, in Freeport, Illinois, published their recipe using yoghurt with their clever title, *Good and Healthy*. Touting it as a 'healthy treat for the youngsters', it's simplistic, but still popular today.

Here's a healthy treat for the youngsters: mix a small can of frozen orange juice with a half-pint of yogurt. Pour into small paper cups, insert pop sticks, and freeze.

Yoghurt and Barley Soup

The Armenian culture have a passion for *matzoon* (yoghurt) and mix it with barley, as people did in ancient days to make this soup recipe, given to me by an Armenian friend, Jill Chavooshian. It dates back to 1905, when her mother-in-law, Marge Chavooshian, learned it from her mother, who was from Sivas. For the Armenian people, who endured a genocide in 1915, it is especially important to keep these age-old recipes alive.

Cook 115 g–170 g (½–¾ cup) of barley in water until soft, about 45 minutes to an hour. Rinse and then strain and cool a bit in the pot. Lightly beat 2 eggs and add that to 950 ml (1 quart) of plain yoghurt. Slowly add the mixture to the barley. Brown 1 large onion that has been chopped with 60 g (½ stick/2 oz) of butter. Add about 2–3 tbsp crushed dried mint and 3–4 tbsp of chopped parsley to the onions. Combine everything and serve. To serve leftovers, add some water to thin out the consistency.

Mango Lassi

A friend of mine born in the Punjab region of India said her home never went a day without a delicious and refreshing glass of lassi. Here's her family's favourite recipe. Makes 1 serving.

240 g (1 cup) plain yoghurt
120 ml (4 oz) milk or water (this is optional; if you prefer a very thick lassi, omit)
180 ml (12 oz) canned mango pulp or the meat from 2 fresh mangoes, stone removed and sliced
1 tbsp sugar, honey or agave, to taste
dash of salt and cardamom
chopped fresh mint (optional)

Place all ingredients in a blender and process about 1 minute or until smooth.

Twenty-first-century Recipes

Beijing Yoghurt

Contributed by Van, www.foodisafourletterword.com

Preparation time: 5 minutes
Cook time: 15 hours
Necessary equipment: Instant Pot

60 ml (¼ cup) plain yoghurt with active cultures
120 ml (½ cup) buttermilk
2 l (65 oz/½ gallon) pasteurized milk
140 g (½ cup + 2 tbsp) granulated sugar

In a bowl, mix 60 ml (¼ cup) plain yoghurt and 120 ml (½ cup) cultured buttermilk with a whisk until the mixture is completely smooth, and there are no yoghurt lumps; set aside. Almost any plain yoghurt will work for this recipe, but I would avoid using Oui and Fage brand yoghurts because they don't get tart enough for this recipe.

Add 240 ml (1 cup) of milk and 140 g (½ cup + 2 tbsp) of sugar to a saucepan or pot. On medium-low heat, stir the milk and sugar until all the sugar is dissolved. This should take about 2–3 minutes. Turn off the heat and pour in the rest of the milk.

Add the yoghurt and buttermilk mixture last; give it a few good stirs with a whisk to ensure the cultures are evenly distributed. Pour the mixture into the Instant Pot and seal the Instant Pot with the lid. Use the yoghurt button and set it for 15 hours, making sure that it's on the 'normal' yoghurt setting. Or use your yoghurt-maker and set it for 15 hours.

If you have the glass bottles, you can incubate the yoghurt in the bottles, the yoghurt ends up being a little thicker, so I prefer this method. Fill the bottles with the mixture and place the bottle caps on them. Place the bottles into the Instant Pot. Use the yoghurt button and set it for 15 hours, making sure it's on the 'normal' yoghurt setting.

Once the yoghurt is done, take the liner out of the Instant Pot and place it in the refrigerator for at least 6 hours. Try to not disturb the yoghurt during this time (don't stir or transfer to another container). If you incubated the yoghurt in the glass bottles, remove the bottles from the Instant Pot and refrigerate for 6 hours.

After it's been refrigerated, transfer to your bottles, jars or cups. Enjoy with a straw.

Serves 6

Labneh with *Zhoug*
Contributed by Kate Burton, chef/proprietor of Cardamom and Dill, a Mediterranean vegetarian restaurant situated in the heart of York, England

Inactive Prep Time: min. 4 hours
Hands on Prep Time: under 30 minutes

For the labneh:
500 g (1¾ cups) of Greek yoghurt, with a generous pinch of sea
salt stirred through
3 cloves of garlic, very finely chopped
1 lemon, zested and juiced

For the zhoug:
30 g (1 oz) coriander
20 g (¾ oz) flat leaf parsley
3 mild green chillies
2 cloves of garlic, crushed
½ tsp ground cumin
¼ tsp ground coriander
¼ tsp sea salt
3 tbsp extra-virgin-olive oil
2 tbsp cold water

To make the labneh, simply stir in the garlic, lemon zest and juice,
and line a sieve with a square of muslin. Place the sieve over a bowl,
and tip in the yoghurt. Bring the corners of the muslin together
and loosely tie. Leave to drain in a cool place for around four hours
(the longer you leave it, the thicker it will become). Keep in the
fridge in an airtight container for up to three days.

For the zhoug, whizz all the ingredients together in a mini
processor until you have the consistency of pesto. It will keep
for about a week in an airtight container, and it freezes well. To
serve, place the labneh in a dish and drizzle with extra virgin olive
oil and the zhoug.

Serves 6–8

Oatmeal Yoghurt Pancakes
Contributed by Wendy Rahamut, Trinidadian cookbook author,
television personality, food stylist, teacher, chef and baker

Prep Time: 10–15 minutes
Cook Time: 3–5 minutes

180 ml (¾ cup) unflavoured yoghurt
120 ml (½ cup) skimmed milk
115 g (½ cup) quick-cooking oatmeal (oat porridge)
1 egg
1 tsp vanilla extract
1 tbsp vegetable oil, or melted butter
280 g (1¼ cups) all-purpose (plain) flour
2 tbsp brown sugar
½ tsp baking soda
2 tsp baking powder
pinch of salt

Combine the yoghurt, milk and oatmeal and let stand for about ten minutes. Beat egg, and add vanilla and oil. Combine flour with brown sugar, baking powder, baking soda and salt. Add the oatmeal mixture to the flour mixture and stir until combined.

Heat a non-stick frying pan; grease with a small amount of butter. Spoon about 80 ml (⅓ cup) of batter onto a hot frying pan and spread gently. When small bubbles appear on the topside of the pancake and the edges look cooked, then flip the pancakes, cook for a short while longer and remove to a plate. Keep pancakes warm while you are cooking the balance. Serve with pancake syrup or maple syrup.

Serves 4

Two-ingredient Yoghurt Dough

Preparation time: 10 minutes
Cook time: 10–15 minutes, depending on use

Making dough is one of life's finest tactile moments, and while I am not one to deprive anyone of this singular pleasure, sometimes you just want a dough that goes quickly and easily, with as few ingredients as possible and little hands-on work. This is that recipe. Using full-fat Greek yoghurt, you are adding creaminess and acidity with a yeasty effect that combines with self-raising flour to make quick work out of a versatile dough. Roll it out for pizza crust, or into balls or breadsticks, or toss it in a hot pan for a fluffy instant naan-like bread. It will be your go-to dough from here on.

280 g (1¼ cups) self-raising flour (if you do not have
self-raising flour, you can make your own: simply
add 1½ tsp of baking powder and ½ tsp of salt per
230 g/1 cup of flour, and mix well)
240 ml (1 cup) plain Greek yoghurt, whole or low fat

Preheat the oven to 220°C (425°F). Mix the two ingredients in a stand mixer, with the paddle or dough attachment, until the dough begins to come together; remove from the mixer and knead on a lightly floured board for about 5 minutes, adding a bit of water if the dough is dry or a little extra flour if it is too tacky. Alternatively, you can use a food processor or simply combine in a bowl. Be sure you knead for about 8 minutes if kneading by hand. No need to let it rise; you can use it right away.

For breadsticks, divide the dough into quarters and then divide each of those in half. Roll out on a lightly floured board into sticks about 20 cm (8 in.) long and place on a baking sheet that is lined with parchment or has been lightly greased. Brush the breadsticks with a touch of olive oil and season with finely chopped dried herbs or sea salt. Bake at 220°C (425°F) for 10–14 minutes. Serve at once.

For naan, heat a cast-iron skillet and add olive oil to lightly coat the bottom of the pan. Divide the dough into four pieces and roll into rounds about 15 cm (6 in.) in diameter. Place each round, one at a time, into the pan and cook quickly, just a minute or two on each side. You can sprinkle on cheese or herbs and salt when they are finished, and serve at once.

If you make the dough ahead of time, wrap it in plastic that has been lightly coated with non-stick spray or oil and refrigerate for up to 2 days.

Serves 4–6

Chicken Biryani

As paella is to Spanish cuisine, biryani is to Indian: flavourful rice melds with warm spices and a range of proteins and vegetables. The yoghurt helps to marinate the meat and create a velvety finish for the dish. Add more or less spice to suit your palate and to create your signature version of this traditional, coveted dish.

Preparation time: 20 minutes
Marinating time: at least 1 hour and up to overnight
Cook time: about 1 hour

For the marinade:
2 tbsp vegetable oil
230 g (1 cup) chopped coriander leaves
115 g (½ cup) chopped mint leaves
6 garlic cloves
2 tsp grated fresh ginger
¼ tsp turmeric
¼ tsp ground cinnamon
½ tsp cayenne (more if you like it hot)
1 tsp ground cardamom
1 tbsp garam masala
1 tbsp cumin
2 tsp ground coriander
2 tbsp sweet paprika
1–2 tsp kosher salt
240 ml (1 cup) plain yoghurt
120 ml (½ cup) water
750 g–1 kg (1.5–2 lb) boneless, skin-on or skinless chicken thighs

For the rice:
2.8 l (3 quarts) water
2 tbsp kosher salt
12 cloves
5 dried bay leaves

8 cardamom pods
1 cinnamon stick
510 g (2¼ cups) basmati rice

For the crispy onions:
2 medium yellow onions, thinly sliced
240 ml (1 cup) neutral oil (such as corn or vegetable)

For the biryani:
120 ml (½ cup) melted ghee or clarified butter
120 ml (½ cup) reserved rice water, warmed in the microwave
1 generous pinch saffron threads

For the marinade, place all the ingredients, except the chicken, in the bowl of a food processor fitted with the metal blade and process until a paste is formed. Remove from the bowl and place in a container to marinate the chicken. Stir in the yoghurt and water. Remove ½ of the marinade and set aside for later. Add the chicken and coat the pieces thoroughly. If marinating for 1 hour, you can leave the chicken out of the fridge; if marinating longer (up to overnight), refrigerate until ready to use, removing the chicken from the fridge 30 minutes prior to cooking. While the chicken marinates, prepare the balance of ingredients.

For the rice, bring water to the boil, along with kosher salt, cloves, bay leaves, cardamom pods and cinnamon stick. Add rice to the boiling water and cook, uncovered, for about 5 minutes – the rice will not be cooked through. Drain (reserving 120 ml/ ½ cup of the flavoured water) and set aside, removing the bay leaves and cinnamon stick. You can leave the cloves and pods, if you want.

The rice can be made 1 day ahead and refrigerated until ready to use. Bring to room temperature before cooking again. Refrigerate the reserved water as well.

For the crispy onions, heat the oil in a large but relatively shallow saucepan. Add the onions and cook over medium heat, stirring often until the onions are lightly browned and crispy. Remove to a paper-towel-lined plate and reserve.

This can be done in batches if your pan is not large enough to hold everything at one time.

To assemble and cook the biryani, melt the ghee/butter and set aside. Place the saffron threads in the warm water and allow to steep while you gather the ingredients to assemble the dish.

Spoon half of the rice into a large sauté pan. Top with half the chicken, along with its marinade, spooning half the reserved marinade on top, drizzling with half of the melted ghee/butter and sprinkling with a third of the crispy onions. Repeat layering with the remaining rice, chicken, reserved marinade, ghee and the next third of the onions. Pour the saffron water over the entire dish. Your goal is to steam the chicken and rice, so cover it and cook on low heat until rice is tender and chicken is cooked through, about 40 minutes. To serve, top with the remaining third of crispy onions.
Serves 4

Raita

Versatile and easy to make, raita is the perfect condiment for everything from chicken and lamb to vegetables.

Preparation time: 10 minutes
Yields 475 ml (2 cups)

1 medium English cucumber, peeled and diced (if using a regular cucumber, peel and then cut lengthwise in half; using a spoon, scoop out the seeds, and then dice)
470 ml (2 cups) plain whole-milk yoghurt
½ tsp of kosher salt
1 tsp ground cayenne, cumin or coriander, or a combination of all three
1 garlic clove, grated
2 tbsp minced fresh mint leaves or coriander

Place the cucumber in a strainer and sprinkle with the kosher salt. Allow the cucumber to drain, rinse, and then dry thoroughly. Add the cucumber to the yoghurt and mix the remaining ingredients. Allow the raita to chill so the flavours meld. Can remain fresh for up to 2 days, but can become a bit watery as it sits, so stir before serving.

Shrikhand

While only three ingredients are truly needed to make this sublimely sweet Indian dessert, you can add a variety of mix-ins to make it your own. Here we've added saffron threads and pistachios for additional flavour and interest.

Inactive preparation time: 8–24 hours
Active preparation time: 10 minutes
Yields 600 ml (2½ cups)

Ingredients
470 ml (2 cups) plain whole-milk Greek yoghurt
1 tbsp warm milk
½ tsp saffron threads
170 g (¾ cup) icing sugar
115 g (½ cup) lightly salted pistachios, roughly chopped
pinch of cardamom powder

To further thicken the yoghurt, place it in muslin and draw the ends together to form a pouch. Tie the bag closed with a rubber band or twist tie. Thread a pencil or hook through the band and suspend the pouch over a strainer, placed over a bowl.

Place yoghurt in the fridge, and let the whey further drain for at least 8 and up to 24 hours. Untie the bag and release the thick yoghurt into a clean bowl. Dissolve the saffron threads in the warm milk and let them steep about 10 minutes. Add the saffron-infused milk and the balance of ingredients to the yoghurt and stir. Cover with wrap and chill. You can sprinkle additional chopped nuts or dried fruit over the top before serving. The *shrikhand* will remain fresh, covered in the fridge, for up to 3 days.

Süzme Yoğurt Tatlisi
(Turkish Semolina-yoghurt Cake with Lemon Syrup)
©Jennifer Abadi, www.JenniferAbadi.com, author of *A Fistful of Lentils: Syrian-Jewish Recipes from Grandma Fritzie's Kitchen* and *Too Good to Passover: Sephardic and Judeo-Arabic Seder Menus and Memories from Africa, Asia and Europe*

Preparation time: 1 hour 15 minutes
Cook time: about 1 hour

For the syrup:
470 ml (2 cups) cold water
680 g (3 cups) sugar
3 tbsp freshly squeezed and strained lemon juice

For the cake:
8 large eggs, separated
115 g (½ cup) sugar
3 tsp lemon zest
230 g (1 cup) fine-grain semolina (pasta flour)
170 g (¾ cup) all-purpose (plain) flour
3 tsp baking powder
375 ml (2 cups) süzme yoğurt (strained Turkish yoghurt) or labneh (strained Middle Eastern yoghurt)
pinch of salt

To serve:
60 g (¼ cup) finely ground pistachio nuts
240 ml (1 cup) süzme yoğurt, labneh, or 120 ml (½ cup) whole-milk yoghurt mixed with 120 ml (½ cup) sour cream

Lightly grease and flour a 25 × 33 x 5 cm (10 × 13 × 2 in.) baking pan, and then keep in refrigerator until ready to use. Preheat oven to 180°C (350°F).

Prepare the syrup: combine the water and sugar in a medium-sized saucepan and rapidly boil it for a full 3 minutes. Lower the heat and simmer it uncovered for about 25 minutes. Remove from heat. Stir in the lemon juice and let the syrup cool at room temperature.

Prepare the cake: in a large mixing bowl, beat the egg yolks with the sugar and the lemon zest until the mixture becomes slightly foamy. Gently fold in the semolina, flour and baking powder, and then the yoghurt. Stir the mixture until well blended. Using an electric mixer, wire whisk or hand-held beater, beat the egg whites until they form firm peaks. Gently fold the egg whites into the semolina and flour mixture. Pour the batter into the pre-pared baking pan and spread it out evenly. Bake it on the centre rack of the oven for 25 to 30 minutes, or just until it becomes a light golden brown and the centre is spongy to the touch.

Serve the cake: remove the pan from the oven, pour the syrup over the squares and sprinkle over the ground pistachios. Let cake cool at room temperature for 30 minutes. Cut it into 12 squares and serve at room temperature with a spoonful of the *süzme yoğurt*, labneh or yoghurt-sour cream mixture on top of each serving.
Serves 12

Yoghurt Semifreddo with Leaf-infused Poached Peaches and Shortbread Crumble

I had the absolute pleasure of preparing this luscious dessert with Jeff Rose, artisan chef, gentleman farmer and cooking instructor at the prestigious Blackberry Farm in Walland, Tennessee. It is company-ready but simple to prepare and delightful to eat on a warm summer day. The bonus was seeing the grass-fed sheep grazing on the farm, whose milk added a rich creaminess to the yoghurt we devoured.

Prep time: about 1 hour,
includes inactive and hands on cooking time

For the semifreddo:
600 ml (2½ cups) heavy whipping (double) cream
3–4 sprigs fresh lemon verbena or basil

180 ml (¾ cup) egg whites (from 6–7 eggs)
340 g (1½ cups) sugar
350 ml (1½ cups) plain Greek yoghurt

For the pecan shortbread crumble:
230 g (1 cup) all-purpose (plain) flour
115 g (½ cup) brown sugar
60 g (½ stick/2 oz) soft butter
60 g (¼ cup) toasted pecans
60 g (¼ cup) toasted coconut
pinch of salt

For poached peaches in leaf-infused syrup:
450 g (2 cups) sugar
450 g (2 cups) water
1 vanilla bean
3–4 fresh fig or peach leaves
5 peaches, quartered
5 fresh figs, quartered

For the semifreddo, heat whipping (double) cream in a saucepan over low heat to a simmer. Add lemon verbena or basil; remove from the heat and allow to steep 30 minutes to an hour. Remove herbs and refrigerate infused cream until thoroughly chilled. Whip until stiff peaks appear.

Bring a pot of water to a boil and turn down to a simmer. Combine sugar and egg whites in bowl and place over the hot pot. Whisking occasionally, bring sugar and egg whites to 70°C (160°F). (The sugar will be completely dissolved.) Place in the bowl of an electric mixer with whipping attachment. Whip until the bottom of the mixing bowl feels room temperature. Meringue will be stiff and shiny and will resemble marshmallow cream.

Gently fold yoghurt into meringue. Fold whipped cream into meringue mixture in two parts, combining quickly to prevent lumps. Spoon mixture into semifreddo moulds or into bowls you want to serve in – your grandmother's teacups work well! Place in freezer for at least 1 hour or until mostly frozen.

For the crumble, toast the pecans and coconut in an oven at 190°C (375°F) for about 5 to 6 minutes or until fragrant. Let nuts cool. Combine sugar, salt and flour together, and slowly rub in the butter. Roughly chop or break pecans, toss them with butter mixture. Bake at 190°C (375°F) for 6–8 minutes or until cookie no longer looks wet and is lightly golden brown on the bottom. Once cool, crumble between fingers. Store in airtight container until ready for use.

For the poached peaches in leaf-infused syrup, whisk together sugar and water and bring to a boil in a saucepan. Remove from heat. Add vanilla bean and fig or peach leaves. Place quartered peaches and 4–5 figs into syrup. Allow to soak in residual heat for 10–15 minutes. Discard leaves. (Rinse off vanilla bean and save for later uses.)

Serve warm peaches and figs around semifreddo and garnish with pecan crumble. Leftover simple syrup can be saved for sweetening tea, pouring over waffles, etc.

Serves 10–12

Beauty Masks

Rima Soni is an internationally known beauty expert who was born in India. She is the author of both volumes of the beauty book *Simply Beautiful*, and she has shared her recipes on how to incorporate yoghurt into your beauty regimen.

Facial Mask

Take 1 tsp yoghurt,1 tsp puréed papaya and ½ tsp honey, mixed with 1 tablespoon powdered rice powder. Apply on face and scrub off after 30 minutes. Rinse with cold water. This mask softens, smooths and brightens skin. Do this three times a week for a healthy, youthful glow.

Hair Mask

Put 2 tbsp yoghurt, 1 banana and 1 tbsp honey in a blender to make a smooth pulp. Massage into hair and scalp. Rinse off after 30 minutes; follow with shampoo. Hair gets a rich conditioning and acquires shine and full body. Do this twice a week for healthy, glossy tresses.

Perfect Pairings

Like bacon and eggs, or rice and beans, some things just go together naturally, each elevating the other. That's clearly the case with yoghurt when you bring another strong and interesting flavour to the mix. Here are some natural combinations.

Yoghurt + seeds = a crunch and satisfying snack. Try chia, pepita, hemp or flax seeds for a healthy midday delight.

Yoghurt + minced herbs = a flavourful dip. From minced mint to chopped coriander, yoghurt takes to assertive herbs masterfully and creates a singular dip for veggies, pita or chips.

Yoghurt + spice = a nuanced condiment. Just about any spice, from warm to nutty, can be stirred into yoghurt to change the flavour. Try a pinch of cumin, coriander, cinnamon or pimenton, and enjoy.

Yoghurt + citrus = a tangy treat. Try zesting a lemon, lime or blood orange, with a squeeze of its juice for good measure for a terrific topping for fish, veggies, lamb and chicken.

Yoghurt + nuts = a protein-packed meal. Ground almonds or pistachios, shredded coconut or trail mix add the perfect crunch to balance yoghurt's silky texture.

Yoghurt + fruit = an obvious choice. Just because it's simple, doesn't mean it's not worth doing. Almost any berry or fruit, from

Adding crunch to yoghurt creates a great texture balance and adds bonus nutrition.

raspberry to açai, grated apple to raisins, gives yoghurt a boost. Stir in a touch of jam or create a compote for an indulgent treat.

Yoghurt + sweetener = a luscious dessert. A drizzle of maple or date syrup, agave or honey balances the tartness perfectly.

Yoghurt + natural extracts = infinite possibilities. Try a few dashes of pure vanilla or almond extract to transform yoghurt into a low-calorie taste explosion.

Yoghurt + veggies = nutrition. Whether you grate fresh carrots or beets, cucumber or radish, you create a terrific accompaniment to meat and poultry dishes.

Yoghurt + alcohol = a grown-up boozy version. A sprinkling of mastiha, grappa or sloe gin adds an adult twist to a humble serving.

Yoghurt loves to be swirled, frozen, warmed and blended, so go ahead and find new and interesting ways to incorporate yoghurt into your diet.

References

Introduction: Yoghurt: A Food Fad Trending for Millennia

1 Yogurt in Nutrition Initiative, 'Yogurt for Health, 10 evidence based conclusions' (2018), p. 11 (author's note, Yogurt in Nutrition Initiative-YINI, is a collaboration between Danone Institute International and American Society for Nutrition).
2 Sreya Biswas, 'Yoghurt and the Functional Food Revolution', BBC News, 6 December 2010.

1 Back to the Future

1 Mark Thomas cited in Adam Maskevich, 'Food History and Culture, We Didn't Build this City on Rock 'n' Roll, It was Yogurt', NPR *The Salt* (16 July 2015).
2 Universität Mainz, 'Spread of Farming and Origin of Lactose Persistence in Neolithic Age', www.sciencedaily.com, 28 August 2013.
3 J. Dunne et al., 'First Dairying in Green Saharan Africa in the Fifth Millennium BC', *Nature*, CDLXXXVI (2012), pp. 390–94.
4 Andrew Curry, 'Archaeology: The Milk Revolution', www.nature.com, 31 July 2013.

5 See 'Feeding Stonehenge: What Was On the Menu
   for Stonehenge's Builders, 2500 BC', UCL News,
   www.ucl.ac.uk/news, 13 October 2015.
6 Susanna Hoffman, *The Olive and the Caper: Adventures in
   Greek Cooking* (New York, 2004), p. 471.

2 'Yoghurtism': A Religious Experience

1 Floyd Cardoz cited in '3 Chefs Talk Diwali and the
   Tradition of Indulging in Sweets', https://guide.michelin.
   com, 7 November 2018.

3 Micro-management

1 Luba Vikhanski, *Immunity: How Elie Metchnikoff Changed the
   Course of Modern Medicine* (Chicago, IL, 2016), ebook, cited
   in Luba Vikhanski, 'The Man Who Blamed Aging on His
   Intestines', https://nautil.us, 19 May 2016.
2 See Luba Vikhanski, *Immunity: How Elie Metchnikoff Changed
   the Course of Modern Medicine* (Chicago, IL, 2016), ebook.
3 Ibid.
4 John Harvey Kellogg, *Autointoxication* [1919] (Arvada, CO,
   2006), p. 313.

4 Yoghurt Goes to Market

1 See Luba Vikhanski, *Immunity: How Elie Metchnikoff
   Changed the Course of Modern Medicine* (Chicago, IL, 2016),
   ebook.
2 View the advert and read the transcript at www.englishecho.
   com/yoghurt, accessed 8 July 2020.
3 'Southland's Yogurt War', *Los Angeles Times*, 21 January 1980.
4 Stephen Logue, 'History of Ski', 18 August 2016, available
   at https://static1.squarespace.com.

5 Culture Shock

1 Dariush Mozaffarian et al., 'Serial Measures of Circulating Biomarkers of Dairy fat and Total Cause-specific Mortality in Older Adults: The Cardiovascular Health Study', *American Journal of Clinical Nutrition* (2018).

2 See the FAQs section at https://ithacamilk.com, accessed 1 July 2020.

3 Nicki Briggs quoted in Elaine Watson, 'Lavva Bets Big on the Pili Nut to Stand Out in the Plant-based Yoghurt Category', www.foodnavigator-usa.com, 31 January 2018.

4 Sarah Von Alt, 'Chobani Announces New Line of Vegan Yogurt Made From Coconut', https://chooseveg.com, 10 January 2019; 'Non-dairy Yoghurt Market Poised to Register 4.9% CAGR through 2027, Globally', www.globenewswire.com, 9 April 2018.

6 Gut Reaction

1 Simin Nikbin Meydani and Woel-Kyu Ha, 'Immunologic Effects of Yogurt', *American Journal of Clinical Nutrition*, LXXI/4 (April 2000), pp. 861–72.

2 B. W. Bolling et al., 'Low-fat Yogurt Consumption Reduces Chronic Inflammation and Inhibits Markers of Endotoxin Exposure in Healthy Women: A Randomized Controlled Trial', *British Journal of Nutrition* (2017).

3 National Research Council, *Carcinogens and Anticarcinogens in the Human Diet: A Comparison of Naturally Occurring and Synthetic Substances* (Washington, DC, 1996).

4 Robin McKie, 'Newly Knighted Cancer Scientist Mel Greaves Explains Why a Cocktail of Microbes Could Give Protection Against Disease', www.theguardian.com, 30 December 2018.

5 J. R. Buendia et al., 'Regular Yogurt Intake and Risk of Cardiovascular Disease Among Hypertensive Adults', *American Journal of Hypertension*, XXXI/5 (13 April 2018).

6 M. Chen et al., 'Dairy Consumption and Risk of Type 2
Diabetes: 3 Cohorts of U.S. adults and an Updated
Meta-analysis', *BMC Med*, XII/215 (November 2014).

7 See www.yogurtinnutrition.com/how-might-yogurt-
influence-weight-and-body-fat, accessed 8 July 2020.

8 'The Brain-gut Connection', www.hopkinsmedicine.org,
accessed 21 August 2020.

9 Rachel Champeau, 'Changing Gut Bacteria through Diet
Affects Brain Function, UCLA Study Shows',
www.newsroom.ucla.edu, 28 May 2013.

10 Didier Chapelot and Flore Payen, 'Comparison of the
Effects of a Liquid Yogurt and Chocolate Bars on Satiety:
A Multidimensional Approach', *British Journal of Nutrition*
(March 2010).

11 April Daniels Hussar, 'Study: Yogurt Makes Mice Slimmer,
Sexier . . . What About Humans?', www.self.com,
8 May 2012.

12 Sgaron M. Donovan and Olivier Goulet, 'Introduction to
the Sixth Global Summit on the Health Effects of Yogurt:
Yogurt, More than the Sum of its Parts', *Advances in
Nutrition*, X/5 (September 2019).

7 Location, Location, Location

1 Madhvi Ramani, 'The Country that Brought Yoghurt
to the World', www.bbc.co.uk, 11 January 2018.

2 See 'Beijing Yoghurt Recipe – Sweet and Tart Drinkable
Yoghurt', https://foodisafourletterword.com, accessed
8 July 2020.

3 Maria Yotova, 'From Bulgaria to East Asia, the Making of
Japan's Yoghurt Culture', *The Conversation*, 30 January 2020.

4 Edith Salminen, 'There Will Be Slime', https://
nordicfoodlab.wordpress.com, accessed 22 July 2020.

8 Homemade Yoghurt: From Formulation to Infatuation

1 Ralph Waldo Emerson, 'Education', in *The Works of Ralph Walso Emerson* [1909], vol. x, available at https://oll.libertyfund.org, accessed 8 July 2020.
2 Claudia Roden, *The New Book of Middle Eastern Food* (New York, 2000), p. 109.

Final Thoughts

1 See '"In Defense of Food" Author Offers Advice for Health', www.npr.org, 1 January 2008.

Websites and Associations

American Society for Nutrition
https://nutrition.org

Cultures for Health
www.culturesforhealth.com

Danone Institute
www.danoneinstitute.org

FOOD Is a Four-letter Word
www.foodisafourletterword.com

Food Navigator
www.foodnavigator-usa.com

Gut Microbiota for Health
www.gutmicrobiotaforhealth.com

International Frozen Yogurt Association
www.internationalfrozenyogurt.com

The Lancet, Elsevier
www.journals.elsevier.com/the-lancet

Medical News Today
www.medicalnewstoday.com

Mintel
www.mintel.com

Newspapers.com
www.newspapers.com

Nice Cup of Tea and a Sit Down
www.nicecupofteaandasitdown.com

Rima Soni
www.rimasoni.com/simply-beautiful.php

Select Bibliography

Cornucopia Institute, 'Culture Wars: How the Food Giants
    Turned Yogurt, a Health Food, into Junk Food'
    (November 2014), available at www.cornucopia.org
Denker, Joel, *The World on a Plate: A Tour through the History of
    America's Ethnic Cuisines* (Boulder, CO, 2003)
Fisberg, Mauro, and Rachel Machado, 'History of Yogurt and
    Current Patterns of Consumption', *Nutrition Review*, LXXIV/I
    (August 2015), pp. 4–7
Fona Institute, 'What's Next for Yogurt: A Global Review'
    (November 2017), available at www.fona.com
Hoffman, Susanna, *The Olive and the Caper: Adventures in Greek
    Cooking* (New York, 2004)
Kurlansky, Mark, *Milk! A 10,000-year Food Fracas*
    (New York, 2018)
Mendelson, Anne, *Milk: The Surprising Story of Milk through the
    Ages* (New York, 2008)
Metchnikoff, Elie, *The Prolongation of Life: Optimistic Studies*
    (New York, 1908)
Rodinson, Maxime, A. J. Arberry and Charles Perry,
    Medieval Arab Cookery: Essays and Translations
    (Los Angeles, CA, 2001)
Toussaint-Samat, Maguelonne, *A History of Food*, trans.
    Anthea Bell (Oxford, 2009)
Uvesian, Sonia, *The Book of Yogurt* (New York, 1978)
Vikhanski, Luba, *Immunity: How Elie Metchnikoff Changed the
    Course of Modern Medicine* (Chicago, IL, 2016)

Yildiz, Faith, *Development and Manufacture of Yogurt and Other Functional Dairy Products* (Boca Raton, FL, 2010)

Zaouali, Lilia, *Medieval Cuisine of the Islamic World: A Concise History with 174 Recipes*, trans. M. B. DeBevoise (Berkeley, CA, 2007)

Acknowledgements

This book – or, for that matter, any of my previous works – would not have been possible without the guidance and support of Andrew F. Smith, my literary guardian angel. I thank him for always having my back and with regard to this project, for suggesting I take my culinary interests in a new direction. Many thanks to the team at Reaktion Books, especially Harry Gilonis, Alex Ciobanu and Amy Salter, who along with Michael Leaman reached across the pond and guided me every step of the way. My first attempts at brewing my own yoghurt owe a debt of thanks to my trusted taste testers (and grandchildren), Henry, Daisy and Aria. They endured watery, thin, too tart, not tart enough batches and eventually gave me six thumbs up, and inspired me to make preparing homemade yoghurt a weekly ritual. Thank you to Michael Neuwirth, Senior Director, External Communication, Danone North America; Siggi Hilmarsson, Founder of Siggi's; Luba Vikhanski, author and expert on the life of Élie Metchnikoff; Evan Sims, founder of Peak Yogurt; Jan Teller, Chief Scientific Advisor, Dystonia Medical Research Foundation; and Jacqueline Dubois, correspondent and liaison for the blog My French Life, for taking time to share insights on yoghurt and its many facets. And no project is ever complete without the love, support and incredible clean-up services of my husband, Ron. When I was knee deep in yoghurt, and everything else I've done for the past 44 years, you have been there to help me find my way.

Photo Acknowledgements

The author and publishers wish to express their thanks to the below sources of illustrative material and/or permission to reproduce it. Some locations of artworks are also given below, in the interest of brevity:

Photo Jennifer Abadi: p. 107; photo Muhammad Irshad Ansari: p. 94 (top); Bibliothèque nationale de France, Paris: p. 31; The British Museum, London: p. 13; photo courtesy Laurie Duncan/barkleydoodles.com: p. 70; photo Anna Frodesiak: p. 116; photo hbieser/Pixabay: p. 27; photos June Hersh: pp. 45, 47, 55, 56, 57, 60, 62, 64, 67, 93, 111, 112, 114, 117, 119, 123; courtesy Christiann MacAuley/stickycomics.com: p. 77; The Metropolitan Museum of Art, New York: pp. 14, 18; photo courtesy Miss Kiki Salon/cardamomanddill.com: p. 104; Nationaal Archief, The Hague: p. 35; The National Photo Collection, Government Press Office Photography Department, Jerusalem: p. 105; courtesy Mariana Ruiz Villarreal: p. 50; photos Shutterstock.com: pp. 6 (sundae-morning), 21 (ozgurshots), 25 (keko64), 61 (Alp Aksoy), 65 (Ievgeniia Maslovska), 69 (JeniFoto), 73 (David Tonelson), 86 (Stoyan Yotov), 87 (Alex-vn), 91 (Dipak Shelare), 92 top (Digi-ConceptInc), 92 foot (StockImageFactory.com), 94 foot (Skilful), 95 (Joanna Wnuk), 97 (Nelladel), 106 (bonchan); photo Marcin Skalij/Unsplash: p. 142; Victoria and Albert Museum, London: p. 12.

Index

italic numbers refer to illustrations; **bold** to recipes